# THE SEVEN QUESTIONS OF
# BUSINESS STRATEGY

### Focus Your Intention
### and Grow Your Business

## Norm Levy

Lakeridge Press

LIBRARY OF CONGRESS CONTROL NUMBER: 2009905109

ISBN 10:  0-9819880-0-8
ISBN 13:  978-0-9819880-0-9

*Cover and Interior Graphics* by Chris Bivins, Spilled Ink Studio
*Content and Copy Editing* by Ann Gosch, byGosch Editorial Services
*Project Management, Content Editing and Layout* by Aliya Nylander, Phew! It's Done™ LLC

# PRAISE FOR THE SEVEN QUESTIONS

*"We used Norm's Seven Questions to form our long-term vision, develop growth strategies, and enhance our board structure."*
—Jeff Lyon, Chairman & CEO, GVA Kidder Mathews

*"Norm provided the planning structure that has been very important to the WAC being rated one of the nation's four best city/athletic clubs."*
—Jim Johnson, President & CEO, Washington Athletic Club

*"The Seven Questions helps you diagnose the issues in your business and develop successful strategies."*
—Russ Goodman, former President, Space Needle Corporation

*"We used The Seven Questions to align every department in our company to our mission, vision and goals."*
—Rich Lacher, CEO, Business Interiors Northwest

*"The Seven Questions is a great tool for every CEO and board member."*
—Steve Johnston, CEO, Landau Associates

*"The Seven Questions has been used to build our international business and our suppliers in India and China are thrilled."*
—Daryl Shamitoff, President, IJC

*"Norm's skill at framing important questions has been a major contributor to our progress in formulating strategic plans."*
—Thomas Brown, former President, Eldec Corporation

*"Your leadership in the concise statement of issues, questions, prioritization and project planning was the best I've seen."*
—George Winn, former CEO, John Fluke Manufacturing

*"Norm's seven-step process on strategies worked extremely well."*
—Liz Otis, former Director, BSC Materiel, Boeing

*"Norm Levy is the best catalyst for organizational success I have ever worked with. He is just exceptional."*
—Edward Kramer, former CEO & Chairman, Synsor Corporation

*"The Seven Questions is a phenomenal primer for strategic decision making in all facets of life: personal, education and business."*
—Darren Levy, IBM Client Executive

To Denise, *my wife* –
who supports my dreams and ambitions;

to Jordan and Avsean, *my sons* –
who make me proud for being who they are;

to Herb and Lydia, *my parents* –
whose love has always been unconditional;

and to Bob, Ray, and Ken, *my brothers* –
who remain my best friends.

*This book is dedicated to you.*

# ACKNOWLEDGMENTS

Writing this book would not have been possible without the incredible support of people on my team. Aliya Nylander deserves extra-special thanks for her strategic vision, project management, research, editing, recruitment of other professionals, and unwavering commitment to quality and on-time completion.

Appreciation goes to David Reinhardt, Dale Freidig, John Campbell, Sally Narodick, Sue Ross, Bill Blake, Arnie Hendricks, Jim Neuburger, and Bruce Jackson for their application and testing of The Seven Questions in strategy work with clients, or for their co-authoring prior books or articles based on The Seven Questions.

A huge thank-you goes to the many clients I have had during the past thirty years, all of whom have applied the concepts I have taught and have achieved greater clarity and company growth as a result. Extra-special thanks go to Howard Behar, former president of Starbucks Coffee, for his friendship and encouragement to develop a business platform around these concepts.

There are two other individuals I wish to thank whom I have yet to meet, though their wisdom inspired me to write this book. Deepak Chopra instilled within me a desire to continually seek clarity in my life and to help others do the same. Wayne Dyer reminded me to pay attention to my own karma, with his advice: "Don't die with your music still in you." This book *is* my music, and I am happy to share it with the world.

# CONTENTS

# PREFACE

## The Challenge

"The world is changing rapidly" is an understatement. The upside-down economy continues to wreak havoc on thousands of businesses each week. Our nation's executives, entrepreneurs, and workforce are anxious to move our economy forward again.

How do we get back to the basics of sound business strategy? What framework of thinking will help us focus our intention on strengthening and creating new business with a renewed sense of purpose and direction? How do we shed our assumptions of the past and begin to rethink our future? As we contemplate this new beginning, how do we formulate a well-orchestrated plan and move with enthusiasm in the right direction?

It is my belief that the difficult answers to these challenges depend on how we frame the questions.

## Who Should Read This Book?

If you are seeking quick answers to the issues you face, you may not find them in this book. If you are seeking questions to guide in-depth thinking about your business or organization, you've come to the right place.

*The Seven Questions of Business Strategy: Focus Your Intention and Grow Your Business* presents a proprietary business planning system called The Seven Questions. I designed this planning framework as a guide for *CEOs and executives* engaged in strategic planning. This framework is also useful for other individuals, including the following:

- *Department heads* use this framework to develop annual strategic and operating plans.

- *Entrepreneurs* use The Seven Questions to help decide which business opportunity to pursue.
- *Board members* review these fundamental questions to ensure they are providing effective governance as fiduciaries to their investors.
- *Business professors* use The Seven Questions as a construct for business planning principles.
- *Venture capital firms and bankers* find The Seven Questions useful for reviewing business plans.
- *Job seekers* use this framework to guide their career decisions.

If you fall within any of these groups, you will benefit from reading this book.

## How to Get the Most Value from This Book

This book poses questions to serve as a catalyst for strategic thinking. You and your team (if you lead a group of people) are the ones who will be doing the thinking, diving deep for those pearls of wisdom.

My role as an author and consultant is to guide you on your journey, to serve as a catalyst for strategic thinking. To help you relate to the concepts presented, I have sprinkled case histories and examples throughout the book. Be reminded, however, that the specific answers you create for your own business must truly come from you and your team to have the impact you desire.

This book is easy to read in one sitting, though I encourage you to meander and take your time. Pause frequently to reflect on your business and how it affects your life and the lives of your employees. Contemplate your own answers to the questions raised.

*Whenever possible, write your answers down on a sheet of paper, or keep a journal on your computer.* The thoughts you capture represent your answers to the most basic questions about your business. See if these answers change over time, or remain the same. Share your answers with others and listen carefully to their feedback.

Apply the questions posed in the book by asking additional, related questions that are more pertinent to your business. The value of this book is only as strong as you make it by customizing the questions to your specific situation.

## Universal Appeal

My clients have ranged from large businesses to small start-ups, representing a broad cross section of industries. Across this span of businesses and organizations, every client has stated that The Seven Questions helped them articulate their vision, manage their critical issues more effectively, and develop strategies to grow their business.

Why such universal appeal over three decades? The reason The Seven Questions works so well in such a vast array of circumstances is that we intuitively reflect on these questions daily. Integrating all questions into one central framework therefore feels quite natural. It creates a meaningful framework for our thinking and is comfortable to remember and to use. This increases the probability of the tool being used on an ongoing basis, which is why this framework "sticks."

# INTRODUCTION

## The Question That Everyone Forgets

Try conducting the same experiment I have conducted since 1978 with predictable results. Ask another person, a small group of people, or even a large audience to prepare a list of the seven one-word questions in our everyday vocabulary. For some reason, people can never remember all seven questions, and the same question is forgotten.

In the early 1980s I was asked to be a guest speaker at the Federal Home Loan Bank with more than one hundred bank executives in attendance.

Conducting my normal routine for introducing my topic of corporate strategy, I wrote the large numbers 1 through 7 in a column on a flip chart pad.

I indicated that strategic and operational planning concepts can be viewed within this easy framework of questions. As an example, I wrote *When* next to the number 7. Then I asked the audience to call out each of the other six questions.

The words were shouted out popcorn style from across the conference room. *"Who!" "What!" "Where!" "Why!"* One by one, I added these four words to the chart.

*"How!"* was then shouted.

I added this last word and then six questions were listed in total.

Then there was dead silence. The audience stared at the board and realized that #2 through #7 were listed, but the #1 question was still missing.

I, too, stared with them and said, "The number-one question is missing."

Stumped, Bruce Baker, a senior bank executive, shouted a request from the back of the room: "Give us a hint, Norm!"

"You want a hint?" I asked.

"Yes," he said.

Others argued, then gave in to hearing the hint.

I stepped back from what had been written and motioned to the entire audience to look at the chart. I said, "There are seven spaces on the board, you have listed six, which is missing."

The room was filled with silence except for Bruce. He exclaimed, "That's no hint, Norm! You said you were going to give us a hint."

Two executives from different sides of the room instantly raised their hands with smiles on their faces. I asked one gentleman to come up to the board and write down his answer. He took the marker from my hand and wrote in big words "How much?"

To his dismay the audience laughed, telling him he was instantly disqualified because his answer had two words instead of only one and he had not followed the instructions. He reluctantly sat down, still proud of himself for being the banker who asked, "How much?"

The second bank executive was a bit nervous as he came up and wrote in big letters "Huh?" After a few chuckles in the audience, someone declared, "That's more of an exclamation than a question." The banker at the podium turned around and very slowly walked back to his seat, still staring at the chart.

Another person asked, "Is the missing question similar to the other six questions?" I replied, "Yes. It is." Someone else asked, "Does it begin with a W?"

I responded by asking, "Well, yes, but do you actually want me to give all of you the answer?" There was a resounding "No!" from the entire audience.

"Then I will repeat what I said earlier. There are seven questions, you have listed six... which is missing."

There was a long, deep silence that seemed to last forever.

"Of what relevance is this little one-word game to our industry?" one bank CEO asked.

"Ah, you want to understand application and relevancy," I replied. "I have already given you the answer and the very future of this industry lies in your collective ability to address this key strategic question."

All of a sudden, three executives stood up at the same time and delightfully shouted, *"Which!"* The audience roared with laughter.

Bruce, a very talented executive with outstanding knowledge of changes in the financial industry, raised his hand again and said, "Norm, your point is well taken. We need to ask ourselves the important question of *which* business we are in, in order to develop growth strategies."

I smiled and said nothing.

Bruce had it right. He had a reputation for being a leader in strategic thinking in the savings and loan industry and knew that *how* the industry defined and differentiated itself would indeed determine the industry's fate.

It seems this single most important question of *which* business one is in determines the fate of most companies and industries.

Along this line, it seems that today's subprime mortgage and credit contraction crisis might not have occurred had there been a more exhaustive questioning of *which* business lenders should be in, *which* types of loans they should have offered, and *which* type of risk they could accept.

This book asks a lot of questions we tend to overlook, yet also teaches a handful of concepts you may find intriguing. Fasten your seatbelt. You are in for a flight of discovery. The trip may not be a smooth one, though you are sure to gain insights and land gracefully.

*Congratulations! Today is your day. You're off to Great Places. You're off and away! You have brains in your head. You have feet in your shoes. You can steer yourself any direction you choose.*
—Dr. Seuss
*Oh, the Places You'll Go!*

# SECTION I

---

## THE FUNDAMENTAL MODEL

*"Everything should be made as simple as possible,
but not simpler."*
—Albert Einstein

# CHAPTER 1:
## Focus Your Intention

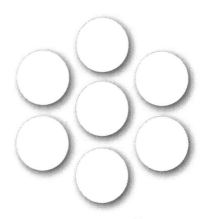

*Our intention creates
our reality.*
—Dr. Wayne Dyer

Imagine taking all of the questions you have about the future of your business and dumping the entire bundle of questions onto the table in front of you. Your job is to organize the pile into a workable framework.

Feel a bit overwhelmed?

Imagine sorting them into *seven* smaller piles, each pile of a different nature.

The task is starting to feel easier, isn't it?

Most people would agree. We can tackle a challenge better if we break it down into smaller pieces. That's exactly what The Seven Questions does and then allows you to integrate them back together again in an organized strategy.

This approach makes planning easier. After studying this model for nearly three decades, I have come to a deep appreciation for its power to help entrepreneurs and executives conceive of new business opportunities. These seven groupings of questions follow a natural order that will be familiar to you.

### The Seven Questions Molecular Model
This model, or conceptual "construct," consists of seven elements that interact with one another in a unique manner.

# THE SEVEN QUESTIONS

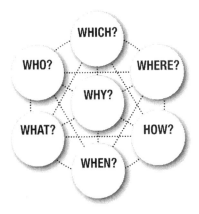

© Copyright 2009 Strategic Development Corporation

*The Seven Questions is the molecular structure of intention, composed of the core elements of inquiry that combine to form strategy.*

These questions reflect *fundamental* elements of thinking. Certain aspects in the universe have such characteristics. The three primary colors of red, blue and yellow, for example, combine to create secondary colors. The three dimensions of space and the ten digits of our numbering system are combinations that possess this same uniqueness.

Such is the uniqueness of The Seven Questions. Each question is distinct. The questions are also able to bond with each other in an intriguing manner. The question *Why* serves as a nucleus and attracts the other six questions into its gravitational field. This phenomenon compels us to look at the reason behind our answers to every question.

Each question can also bond with other questions. For example, alternative growth paths that are strategic choices (derived from the question *Which*) can be resolved by considering decision criteria (derived from the question *Why*). Another example is *what* you want to achieve as a goal becomes more meaningful when you couple it with *how* and by *when?*

## The Elements of Intention

The Seven Questions reflect seven fundamental elements of intention: choice, purpose, position, people, results, process, and action.

# Elements of Intention

© Copyright 2009 Strategic Development Corporation

In business, this means making the right choices for the right reasons, having the right leaders who position your brand uniquely in the marketplace, and having clear goals, strategies and accountability for taking action.

These seven elements represent the "derivatives" of The Seven Questions. For example, the subject of choice is derived from the question *Which*. The subject of people is derived from the question *Who*. And so forth. Choice, purpose, position, people, results, process, and action are the seven Elements of Intention™ that are derived from The Seven Questions.

At first, when you look at The Seven Questions your immediate reaction might be, "Well, so what? What's the big deal about these?" It is when you focus your intention on the elements reflected by the questions that their combined importance presents a powerful model for crafting strategy.

# THE SEVEN QUESTIONS
## Elements of Intention

© Copyright 2009 Strategic Development Corporation

If you run your business with continued respect and caring for these seven elements, your business will grow. These themes can also be used as both a diagnostic tool and audit tool to evaluate the strategic effectiveness and operational efficiency of your business.

It is when we forget the lessons of each question and their corresponding element that businesses become off-balance. Just as personal health is a matter of balance, business health is also a matter of balance. *How* do we maintain such balance?

By focusing our intention on the elements that combine to form strategy help ensure we give appropriate weight to each, thereby creating better balance.

This may sound like mumbo jumbo, but have you known of a business that had the right market strategy, but not the right people? Or one that had chosen the right customer segment to pursue, but delivered the wrong product? Have you observed a business that invented a better technology, but failed to capture as much market share as its competitor that had a less effective technology?

The list of examples of businesses that failed to answer all questions goes on and on. If you execute these fundamentals well, your business will likely grow and be successful. If you fall short on any of these key themes, or do not align your business to this framework, your results may not be as impressive as you would have hoped. It is actually that simple.

This book serves as a catalyst to crystallize your strategic thinking about your business. It is my hope that by reading *The Seven Questions of Business Strategy* and applying its principles, you will successfully:

**Focus Your Intention
and Grow Your Business.**

# SECTION II

---

## THE STRATEGIC QUESTIONS

*"Management is doing things right;*
*leadership is doing the right things."*
—Peter Drucker

## Strategic Effectiveness and Operational Efficiency

In The Seven Questions Framework, the questions *Which, Why, Where,* and *Who* generally address strategic matters; I refer to these as the *strategic effectiveness* questions. *What, How, and When* address operational matters; these are the *operational efficiency* questions.

### THE SEVEN QUESTIONS™ FRAMEWORK
#### Components of Intention

| | Question | Element | Conveys |
|---|---|---|---|
| **Strategic Effectiveness** | 1. Which? | Choice | Niche |
| | 2. Why? | Purpose | Values |
| | 3. Where? | Position | Vision |
| | 4. Who? | People | Culture |
| **Operational Efficiency** | 5. What? | Results | Goals |
| | 6. How? | Process | Method |
| | 7. When? | Action | Timing |

This framework links each question with its corresponding element of intention and business concept conveyed by each element. It also illustrates the difference between strategic and operational questions.

Peter Drucker has been credited for noting an important distinction between operational efficiency and strategic effectiveness. From his view, which I share, operational efficiency represents doing things right; strategic effectiveness addresses doing the right things. Remember this very important lesson and the distinction between these categories of questions. Doing so will serve you well in diagnosing critical issues and developing strategies to grow your business.

## Become Strategically Effective

What does "doing the right things" really mean? If this concept is so important, how do we do more of it?

Doing the right things extends from choosing *which* business niche to pursue, *which* products and services to offer, *which* distribution channels to use, and *which* strategic alliances or mergers are appropriate to grow your business. Being strategically effective means carefully positioning your business for long-term growth.

Strategic questions address the purpose and mission of your business, providing a sense of *why* your business exists for the benefit of all stakeholders. Strategic effectiveness requires that your market position and long-term vision are clear and that there is an understanding of *where* your industry is headed.

Being strategically effective, calls for a deliberate positioning of *who* your business is as a brand. It requires a deep understanding of the people and leadership elements in creating a healthy work culture.

For all of these reasons, pay close attention to the following chapters on strategic questions as they apply to growing your business.

# CHAPTER 2: WHICH?
## The Element of Choice

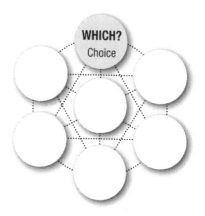

*Destiny is not a matter of chance;*
*it is a matter of **choice**.*
—William Jennings Bryan

## The Essence of *Which* Conveys Choice

The question Which implies a choice among alternatives. The operative word is *choice*. The act of choosing suggests a brain activity resulting in either a conscious or unconscious decision to make a selection. Conscious choice is an important element in life that makes us feel alive. Being aware of the choices we make each moment gives us that feeling of empowerment.

How we answer the question Which in our personal lives can have a profound impact: which person we choose to marry, in which location we choose to live, and which career we choose to pursue. Making the right choices can greatly affect the rest of our lives.

Yet how often do we exclaim to ourselves in frustration, "*How* did I get to be in this situation to begin with?" If you think back, you will be able to trace your current situation to key choices you made in your past. The same is true in business.

"*Which* business are you in?" can be an intriguing question. *How* you define your business gives rise to the brand, culture, and future thinking about which services and products to offer or to not offer.

In his article "Marketing Myopia" in *Harvard Business Review,* Ted Levitt illustrated this question by noting that the railroads lost their way when they incorrectly defined themselves to be in the railroad business rather than the transportation business. The railroads were product-oriented rather than customer-oriented. Sticking only with what they then defined as their core business, the railroads lost tremendous market share in interstate commerce when highways were constructed and the trucking industry soared.

This is a familiar example to most businesspeople and often overused, yet it teaches lessons we so often forget. Ironically, with fuel prices skyrocketing and taking their toll on the trucking industry, railroad companies once again have an opportunity to gain market share.

## Case History: Starbucks

During the early 1990s I was fortunate to serve as a strategy consultant to Starbucks. The process began with a strategy retreat at Battelle Conference Center in Seattle and led to weekly meetings with a newly formed Executive Committee.

One day as the executives were discussing their sale of coffee to Costco, I asked the question "*Which* business are we in?" Orin Smith, the CFO, answered that Starbucks' business was to sell premium coffee and even though Costco was not a Starbucks retail coffeehouse, there would be synergies beneficial to growth. Besides, he said, it fit their mission statement: "Purveyors of the finest coffee in the world." (Starbucks' new mission is "To inspire and nurture the human spirit—one person, one cup, and one neighborhood at a time.")

Months passed. In another meeting Howard Behar, the president, raised the subject of the product line the stores were offering. Once again, to help develop and align strategies, I asked, "*Which* business are we in?" Howard Schultz, the CEO, exclaimed, "We've already answered that question, Norm. We are purveyors of the finest coffee in the world."

Howard Behar urged the team to focus deeply on my question and said, "We are going to have to continually address this important question if our brand is going to evolve. Since the market continues to change, if we don't continue to reinvent ourselves, we will not achieve our goals." Howard Schultz, who prided himself in being the keeper of the brand, smiled because he knew Howard Behar's thinking would help Starbucks evolve.

At that time, there was not much to buy in a Starbucks store other than coffee beans and espresso drinks. Howard Schultz said, "I do not want to become a convenience store and offer everything. We have a brand to build." How right he was.

During the following ten years, Starbucks continued to reshape its brand by the relentless pursuit of "*Which* business are we in?" The product offerings grew to include baked goods. Some of the chairs changed from being hard seats to soft couches with cushions to relax for hours. In a few stores, even fireplaces were added. The question of "*Which* business are we in?" was examined constantly, changing the brand from merely a place to get a great cup of coffee to a great place where people simply wanted to *be*—a "*third place*" after home and work.

Today Starbucks sells a broad array of carefully selected products as diverse as coffee brewing equipment and music CDs. Has its sense of *which* business it is in changed over time? Without question it has. Starbucks has not only continued to reshape itself, it has reshaped American culture.

## Challenge Your Business or Face the Consequences

Steve Miller, a successful entrepreneur and friend, told me that his father invented the 8-track tape player. I am old enough to remember how revolutionary this was at the time this invention came onto the market. The solution solved the challenge of a magnetic reel-to-reel continuous play. But it wouldn't be long before digital technologies would replace an analog technology even as it was being perfected. The 8-track tape player had a relatively short life span.

Can you think of other industries in which new technologies, products, or services have displaced former businesses?

I once helped Software Production, Inc. sell its business that mass produced software on 5¼-inch disks and 3½-inch diskettes in a highly efficient manner for companies like Microsoft. Not only did this business focus on a short-term opportunity, but its logo even reflected a 5¼-inch disk. There is risk in a company's defining itself by its product instead of the generic value it provides to its market.

The following analogy is timeworn yet still insightful. Suppose your business was a premier manufacturer of drill bits. If I asked you which business you are in, you might respond: "We manufacture high-quality drill bits." I might ask you to think of the generic function your business provides to your customers. Then your answer might be: "We are in the hole-making business."

This realization might lead to further questions, such as: Which other products or services should you consider selling to enable your customers to make holes better, faster or cheaper? Diamond-tip bits to be more durable? Water-jet cutters? Laser-jet cutters?

You get the point. The key is to ask the question from the perspective of your customer or end user of your product, and not from your own perspective. This may yield a completely different answer to help define your business and your mission.

How do you define which business you are in? Take a moment to write down your answers in your strategy journal.

Begin with the obvious and continue the process until you discover the true value that keeps your customers coming back. Then discuss this with your most important customers to get some feedback. You'll find out the truth.

When I served as a keynote speaker for an audience of CPAs, I asked them *which* business they were in. Their answers were diverse: auditors, financial advisors, management consultants, and purveyors of accurate financial information. My view is that there may be a difference between seeing yourself as a financial advisor and seeing yourself as someone who helps your clients increase their net worth and manage risks. How you perceive *which* business you are in may influence *how* you approach customers and grow your own business.

### Case History: Herman Miller

I am currently helping Herman Miller Inc., a leading manufacturer of office furniture, and some of its independent dealers in developing growth strategies. I often ask the dealers I work with, "*Which* business are you in?" While dealers sell furniture systems, the responses to my question vary based on the markets they are serving.

Some define their business as creating the right ambience for their corporate customers to be more inspired, energized and productive. Others who sell furniture to hospitals see their business as improving patient outcomes. Other salespeople who sell furniture to educational institutions see their business as enhancing the learning environment.

Notice that each answer focuses on the true value they are delivering to their specific type of customer. I consider this an important element of strategic selling in that their level of customer care goes far beyond focusing on just the product being sold.

## Case History: Kibble & Prentice

To effectively identify which business you are in, you may need to look past the description of your product or service being sold and discover the underlying motives of your customer.

Arnie Prentice, a client and friend, is chairman of the Seattle insurance and investment firm Kibble & Prentice, now a subsidiary of USI Holding Corporation. The firm has grown steadily over many years, and its reputation for honesty and integrity is stellar. In fact, Kibble & Prentice won awards in 2005 and 2006 from *Washington CEO* magazine as one of the Best Places to Work.

When I asked Arnie *which* business he was in, his response was "we help people manage risks." Risk management is an excellent answer that addresses a fundamental reason that clients purchase insurance. When I then asked the question, "What value do your clients get when their risks are managed?" Arnie's response was again brief: "peace of mind." Now, there's clarity! What a price each of us would pay to have more peace of mind.

## Case History: Cinnabon

Years ago I had the wonderful experience of working with Cinnabon, the company known for its world-famous cinnamon rolls. Dennis Waldron, its founder and first CEO, once said, "We don't just sell cinnamon rolls; we sell the ability for people to reward themselves." I found that to be very insightful.

In meetings with senior management, we devoted months to identifying the most important emotional response of a customer's first bite into a freshly baked Cinnabon cinnamon roll. We settled on one single word that said it best: "Wow!" This captured the team's passion for the impact they wanted to make.

From that point forward, all Cinnabon products had to pass the rigorous "Wow response test" in order to be considered worthy of company support. This led to years of formulating and retesting Cinnabon's new hand-held snack before releasing it to market.

## Case History: The Space Needle

The Space Needle is a terrific success story in Seattle and well-known throughout the world. Years ago Russ Goodman, the company's president, hired me as a strategy consultant. Since its early beginnings at the 1962 World's Fair, the Space Needle has always done well as a tourist attraction. As good as business seemed to be, the Wright family, who built the structure and own the business, was curious whether earnings could shoot still higher.

Russ took on the board's challenge. Through a series of intense strategic meetings with his staff, the team came up with a new angle. Everyone knew that local residents would bring their out-of-town guests to the Space Needle, but the question was how to have them come back even without their out-of-town guests.

The Space Needle executive team created a new view of *which* business they were in: special occasions. Their advertising campaign was changed to include a new jingle about special occasions. After 18 months, Russ wrote a thank-you note saying, "The Space Needle has achieved results never before realized in its history." I was honored to work with a terrific team of people.

Considering the simple question *"Which* business are we in?" from the viewpoint of the value to the customer can reveal substantial opportunities you may not have thought about before.

## Critical Issues Occur at Any Time

I define a critical issue as "a threat or opportunity that poses a substantial impact on performance."

When do critical issues occur? The answer is "issues happen" (similar to another expression you might be familiar with). This means they can occur at any time, sometimes without advance warning. Because we now live in a more dynamic world ecosphere, events that happen around the world bring about changes in economic, regulatory, competitive, and technological forces quite frequently. A terrorist event can dramatically affect businesses overnight, as we have seen.

For these reasons, executives are now shifting their internal culture and attitude toward strategic planning. Strategic planning is no longer viewed as just an annual exercise of extrapolating future financial results, but rather an exercise driven by a need to manage critical issues. Senior executives in many firms are now routinely engaging in strategic thinking on an ongoing basis to manage critical issues.

## Critical Issues Management

I view one of the primary purposes of strategic planning to be an ability to better resolve critical issues. How do you develop strategic plans that resolve critical issues, while reflecting your strategic intent (mission, values, vision and goals)?

The answer is what I refer to as *critical issues management*. This is the process of identifying and managing critical issues whereby strategic decisions are aligned with strategic intent and drive the development of strategic and operating plans.

A good starting point is to conduct a situational analysis. You may uncover more than fifty important issues that need to be addressed. This would be overwhelming to most.

To make things more manageable, determine *which* of these issues are most critical by assessing the magnitude of potential impact on your company. Most likely, only a few issues are really critical or perhaps only one issue. By managing critical issues, you are more likely to create substantial benefit from an opportunity to be pursued or a risk to be avoided.

## CRITICAL ISSUES MANAGEMENT
### Manage Issues by Aligning Decisions with Intention

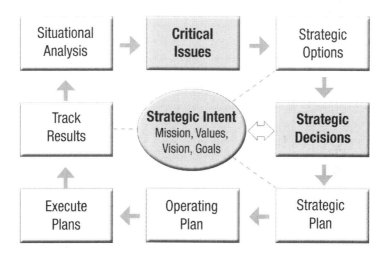

Once the critical issues have been identified, determine whether there are issues that pose major strategic options facing your business. For example, suppose your options are important choices such as:

- Choice of *which* business to be in.
- Choice of *which* products to target.
- Choice of *which* alliances to develop.

To resolve these strategic options, the next step is to determine the decision criteria that are relevant to each type of choice. Having criteria will help determine the basis on which the decision would be made. (Formulating decision criteria is discussed in more depth in Chapter 3: Why).

Be sure to consider how a given alternative would be supported by the strategic intent of your business (vision, mission, values and goals). By comparing potential decisions with your existing strategic intent, four types of outcomes are possible:

1. The decision is directly supported by your company's strategic intent.
2. The decision is *not* supported because it would cause departure from your strategic intent.
3. The decision is sound, but your strategic intent would need to be adjusted or broadened to enable alignment.
4. The strategic intent is sound, yet the decision must be modified in some way to ensure alignment.

After aligning the potential strategic decisions with your strategic intent statements, you are now ready to incorporate your conclusions in your long-range strategic business plan.

The time frame for a strategic plan is generally three to five years for most industries or even longer for some. The time frame you choose to use may be shorter or longer depending on how rapidly change is occurring in your industry.

*Freedom is the right to choose; the right to create*
*for oneself the alternatives of **choices**.*
—Archibald MacLeigh

## Which Are Your Most Critical Issues?

One of the most vital functions of leadership is to *choose* the single, or critically few, issue(s) that have a substantial impact on your business.

Try doing this exercise for your business: Identify a critical issue (remember, this is either a threat or opportunity that could have a substantial impact on your company's performance). Write down the most critical issue that comes to mind. Next address *why* this is a critical issue. What is so important about this issue? How could the impact of this issue either "make or break" your company? What risk exists if the company fails to manage the issue?

In some organizations (hopefully not yours), there are certain subjects that may have a huge impact on your business but that have not been placed directly on the table to discuss. These are the "elephants in the room" that haven't yet been exposed and may be at the heart of a problem. Attempt to reveal these elephants so that your team can truly address the source of a critical issue.

For example, at a financial institution, the senior managers knew the president had a drinking problem because of his behavior on Monday mornings. Yet, as senior managers discussed an upcoming all-employee meeting to be held on a Monday, at which the president was to be a guest speaker, no one wanted to express their fear of a potential disaster, even as their faces betrayed what was really on their mind. This huge issue was clearly in the room, yet remained unspoken.

You may also have a situation where certain assumptions have been set in place that nobody wants to challenge for fear of reprisal by someone in authority. For example, the founder and CEO of a manufacturing company continually received praise for providing the industry with the highest quality device. The company was also losing market share year after year to competitors that produced similar equipment at a lower cost. The engineers were always chastised by the CEO whenever they suggested manufacturing another line of products that were not as high in quality, but that may have helped the company grow and be successful. While investors complained of a poor return on equity, the CEO stated that their reputation for quality was more important than earnings. This revealed a conflict of values between investors and management.

Strive to foster a company culture in which *any* issue can be placed on the table. Nothing should be unreasonably immune from criticism or opposition. There should be no "sacred cows," with the exception of strong values like integrity.

> *The only sacred cow in an organization should be its basic philosophy of doing business.*
> —Thomas Watson Jr.

By definition, the most critical issues of your business are fundamental to your future performance. Issues often reveal major *choices* your business faces. Be careful to identify the major alternatives you could pursue to better manage each choice.

For example, if a critical issue is your product line, write down the various products you now offer or could offer in the future. If the issue is deciding which markets to target, write down the alternative markets you are considering. If the issue is who should run your company, write down the names of possible candidates.

If the issue is creating strategic alliances, write down the alternative businesses under consideration. If the issue is creating a liquidity event for your investors, write down the potential exit strategies for achieving this outcome. These all represent strategic choices you may face.

## Alternative Strategies to Grow Your Business

Consider the alternative strategies you have to grow your business in terms of your product line and target markets. Between existing and new products, and existing and new customers or markets, there are four distinct strategy choices, as shown in the following chart.

## STRATEGIC CHOICES
### Alternatives Strategies to Grow Your Business

**Products or Services**

|  | Existing | New |
|---|---|---|
| **Existing** | Sell more existing products and services to existing customers. | Develop and sell new products or services to existing customers. |
| **New** | Sell existing products and services to new customers. | Develop and sell new products or services to new customers or new markets. |

*Customers or Markets*

© Copyright 2009 Strategic Development Corporation

The easiest path to growing your business is represented in the upper left-hand quadrant—selling more existing products and services to your existing customers or markets. This path is easiest because it does not require either development of new products or pursuit of new market segments with which you may be unfamiliar. It represents sticking with the familiar and is therefore relatively low risk.

The quadrant in the top right reflects developing new products and services for your existing market. Many executives consider this as being customer or "market driven." This means understanding the needs of your customers and market segments and delivering products to meet their needs. Risk is increased because you are now selling something new, which not only your sales force but also your customers need to learn.

The lower-left quadrant represents being "product driven," in which you find new customers and markets for your existing products. For example, this may mean either growing your business by pursuing new geographic markets or pursuing new market segments that have different demographic characteristics.

The lower-right quadrant reflects the broadest answer to the question *which* business are we in by enlarging the scope to develop new products and services for new markets. This segment requires the highest degree of entrepreneurship because the activities are new to your business. For these reasons, this path also entails the highest degree of risk.

If you are seeking either equity or debt capital to fund the growth of your business, understanding the types of risk associated with each path is important. Whether you are discussing funding with your bank, angel investors, or venture capital firms, seek to understand the tolerance of risk your specific audience can comfortably fund.

Additional questions you may wish to examine include the following:

- Which growth path is best for your business during each stage of growth?

- Which growth path would yield the highest results from your sales team?
- What is the level of funding needed for the path you are choosing and how long will it take to recoup the initial investment?
- Which path reflects the appropriate balance of risk and reward that you desire?

These questions reveal major choices you have in growing your business. What other questions are pertinent to your situation from the standpoint of considering the interests of all stakeholders?

## Choices for Your *Current* Business

Every organization has fundamental choices it must make about its niche or charter. The following ten questions may be helpful in defining your business and strategies. Write down short answers here or in your journal and encourage others on your team to do the same, and then compare notes.

1. *Which* business are we in?


2. *Which* services or products do we currently offer?


3. *Which* geographic regions do we currently operate in?


4. *Which* market segments do we currently target?

5. *Which* competitive position does our brand currently represent?

6. *Which* distribution channels do we currently use to sell our products or services?

7. *Which* business segments should we expand?

8. *Which* business segments should we reduce or eliminate?

9. *Which* issues are currently most critical?

10. *Which* organizational structure design best fits our current business model?

Now list a few more questions that specifically deal with major choices you are currently facing. These may be more pertinent to the growth of your business than the generic questions already listed. Repeat the process of comparing the answers each team member gives, and then see if you can reach consensus.

## Choices for Your *Future* Business

After completing the preceding exercise, envision that it is five to ten years into the future. How has your business evolved?

Consider the same questions and, though you may not know all of the answers at this time, try your best at writing down the answers that appear to be attractive *in the future.*

1. *Which* business will we pursue?

2. *Which* services or products will we offer?

3. *Which* geographic regions will we operate in?

4. *Which* market segments will we target?

5. *Which* competitive position will our brand represent?

6. *Which* distribution channels will serve our business?

7. *Which* new business segments will we enter?

8. *Which* segments will we no longer do business in?

9. *Which* critical issues will we face?

10. *Which* organizational design will fit our business model?

> *Our lives are a sum total of the*
> ***choices*** *we have made.*
> —Dr. Wayne Dyer

## Relationship of Choices in Business and Life

The essence of choice is fundamental in business as well as in life. Sometimes one affects the other. Consider your own answers to the following questions:

1. *Which* career have I been pursuing and how will that change as the business I am in changes?

2. *Which* geographic area do I live in now and in which area do I want to live in the future, or to which area am I willing to move if the right business opportunity presents itself?

3. *Which* community activities do I currently engage in and how do those create business opportunities for me?

4. *Which* individuals do I choose to have in my circle of friends and business acquaintances?

5. *Which* recreational activities do I enjoy the most right now, and which ones would I enjoy in the future that would help generate more business?

As you make choices in business, ensure that you have thought through the impact on your life and your family. In this manner, you are more apt to make the best overall choices. Here are some examples where I have observed that a business choice was intertwined with an impact on someone's life, or vice versa.

**Case A:** The board of directors of a company deliberated for months whether to expand their business to an adjacent state. Substantial market evaluation and financial analysis was conducted. After the board decided to open the out-of-state office, they asked all of the managers if any of them would be willing to move to open up the new office. Each of the managers had children in school and no one wanted to relocate. The board decided that hiring someone new to open another office was not the answer. The decision to expand was abandoned, but thousands of dollars on the analysis and pending expansion had been wasted. The board had never considered the question of impact on their employees' lives.

**Case B:** A management consultant reported outstanding financial results year after year. He boasted to his colleagues how many days he spent on the road and how much his income had risen. During this time his wife and children continued to distance themselves from him because of his constant absence from soccer games, school functions, and other family events. His priorities shifted after his marriage almost ended in divorce.

## Key Lessons of This Chapter

1. *Which* is a question that implies *choice.* The key choices you have in business reflect fundamental decisions, such as how you define *which* business you are really in; *which* products, services, or distribution channels to pursue (or to *not* pursue); *which* alliances are most important; and *which* brand position to adopt in your market. Another important choice is to decide *which* issues are most critical to resolve.

2. Most businesses forget that they have these choices, and they make the incorrect assumption that yesterday's choices will serve them well tomorrow. Don't make this mistake! Always identify all of the choices you have.

3. Remain conscious of your choices. Doing so unveils the power you truly have to constantly reevaluate your business and to make decisions accordingly. If you fail to identify the key choices your business has, you may not recognize opportunities in front of you. Start raising your antennae on the choices that are always present.

## Actions to Take

1. Jot down every important choice facing your business.

2. Note *which* choices for which you are confident you have the necessary information for resolution, and *which* choices require more research for your management team or board of directors to resolve.

3. Jot down *which* forces you can influence and which ones you cannot. Then focus your attention on that which you can influence.

## You're Making Progress

By now these questions should have helped you identify the choices you are facing and enabled you to come up with some tentative answers. If so, congratulations are in order. This key step you've made reflects an increased awareness on your part and progress toward crafting your intention. Let's summarize your progress:

You have reexamined your niche and alternative **choices** and have gained new insight into *which* business to be in, *which* market to target, *which* products and services to sell, and *which* distribution channels to use.

At the conclusion of each chapter we will recap the progress you have likely made to that point. At each progress list, pause to add notes as desired to help you continue your quest for clarity.

Not yet experiencing any epiphanies? Take heart! The next chapter examines the purpose and motives behind the decisions you make. Understanding your purpose in *why* you make the decisions you make can be framed as decision criteria. This can help you refine your business model and thereby help you gain new insight about your business niche.

# CHAPTER 3: WHY?
## The Element of Purpose

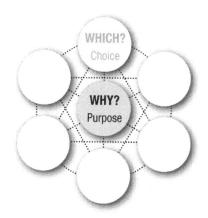

*He who has a why to live for can
bear almost any how.*
—Friedrich Nietzsche

## The Essence of *Why* Conveys Purpose

Underneath the question *Why* lies our purpose, motive, reason, values, or cause that drives us to the choices we make. *Why* reflects an intended outcome we are seeking. Raising the question *Why* evokes introspection. Most of us express a hope that the choices we make reflect the values we hold. Sometimes we discover this is not the case.

At times we find ourselves making choices for some reason not immediately apparent. Sometimes the questions posed by a skilled therapist can help us get at the underlying purpose in our lives to better understand and appreciate ourselves.

The same is true in business. If we are able to identify and embrace the true purpose of our business, we are in a better position to strengthen decisions and company performance. This book was written about the compelling questions I have posed to many of my successful clients in the hope that you, as a business executive, will find value in pondering the answers as they apply to your own business.

## Uniqueness of the Question *Why*

*Why* is unique in relation to the other six one-word questions in that it is often asked at a level secondary to another separate, primary question. For example, *Which* business are we in and *why*? *Where* are we headed and *why*? *What* are we going to achieve and *why*? Thus, answering the question *Why* provides insight to the purpose we seek in answering all other questions.

As a secondary question, *Why* goes beyond what the other six questions ask. While each of the other six questions can be answered with succinct content (choice, position, people, results, process, and action), the question *Why* challenges us to address the rationale behind our thinking.

As a primary question, *Why* can be one of the most difficult questions to answer. "*Why* do I exist?" seems to be one of those rare questions we continue to ask throughout life. "*Why* do we exist as a business?" is a question that evokes the most intense discussions among executive teams, entrepreneurs, and board members.

### Case History: "Which Business Are We In and Why?"

A young CEO of a savings and loan institution once engaged my services to pose questions of strategy so the institution could get a "strategic perspective." In a board meeting I attended, the chairman, a 94-year-old gentleman, who presided over a board of seven with an average age of 83, seemed perturbed. He was not delighted that his new, young CEO had hired another consultant just after a very large national consulting firm had prepared a lengthy analysis of how to improve profitability.

The chairman grunted, "I don't understand why we should hire another consulting firm after paying such a large sum to the last consulting firm to help us improve our profitability. How can you (pointing to me) do better than this?" He slid a very thick report across the conference table at me.

I flipped through the report quickly, seeking to find an example that might demonstrate the value of strategic effectiveness versus operational efficiency. I said, "This is excellent work. Your consultants have recommended how to do the right things to improve your operational efficiency and lower your expenses. If you follow their recommendations, profits should improve."

"So what else is there?" the chairman asked gruffly.

"There are always other ways to improve profits," I said. Borrowing from Peter Drucker's observations, I pointed out, "You have examined operational efficiency and doing things right. Strategic effectiveness and doing the right things are also important."

"Give me an example," he said inquisitively.

I opened the book of recommendations prepared by this large consulting firm. "Well, here for example," I began, "is a recommendation to re-price your N.O.W. accounts. Why do you have these accounts?" I asked.

"These accounts," the vice president of savings said proudly, "are Negotiable Order of Withdrawal accounts that enable the savings and loan industry to offer checking accounts, giving institutions like us the ability to compete head-to-head with banks."

I asked the chairman, "*Why* do you want to compete with the banks in this community? Who are you as a brand? How are you perceived?"

I will never forget his answer. He shook his head with utter confidence in his knowledge and shrugged when he said, "Eh."

"Eh?" I asked. He responded that he felt they were an average institution, no better and no worse than any other in the area. I asked a follow-up question: "How do you know this?"

"Son," he said, "I've been in my position longer than you have been alive. I know *exactly* how this community feels about us and it is simply not a big deal."

"Well, your brand position is a very important piece of information," I responded, "because *if* the community feels stronger about your institution, maybe there's no need to compete with the banks by having an account that requires drive-up windows and envelopes. Your method of competing is expensive and the question is, Why do you feel a need to compete? Is there not a niche you can occupy and do very well in without competing with giant banks?"

"Your point is well-taken, young man," he conceded, looking at the chief financial officer, who had repeatedly challenged the vice president of savings on this very subject.

In a subsequent meeting we agreed to hire a well-known market research firm to conduct a survey of residents in the area, posing the question: "Of the following ten financial institutions in your community, which institution do you trust the most?"

The answer was astounding. Not only was my client not perceived as "eh," but on the contrary, this institution was perceived at the top of the list on the basis of trust.

This translated into a business opportunity to offer services requiring a high level of trust. The client began pursuing the business of offering mortgage insurance for its customers with home loans.

Soon the need to compete with major banks became less important because the institution was strengthening its new profit centers. N.O.W. accounts were no longer perceived to be so vital as "loss leaders" and were priced accordingly.

There are many questions this case history raises, among them: *Why* does your business offer the products and services it offers? *What* specific reasons do you have and which assumptions are you making about your marketplace? *Which* decision criteria do you use when deciding to add or drop a line of business and *why?*

## Why? Why? Why?

Another fascinating aspect of the question *Why* is the ability to repeat the same question to any answer that is presented. To see what I mean, suppose I asked you: "*Why* are you in the business you are in?"

You might respond with many different answers, such as "We are the experts at doing this" or "We make money at this" or "The Board decided" or "We got into this because our competitors forced us into it." Etcetera.

I could then repeat the question *Why* as in "*Why* is that?" You would then apply the question *Why* to your previous answer, thinking of a reason underlying the answer you had just given. In short, this approach causes you to dig deeper and deeper, gaining additional insights. When you get to Chapter 11, Dig Deeper, additional insights are provided on the art of asking questions.

Try this for yourself. Pose the question *Why* to any subject about yourself or your business. After you give an answer, ask the same question *Why* again. Repeat asking yourself *why* after each answer you give and see where your answers take you. Besides being fun, it's interesting to see *why* you do what you do and maybe learn more about yourself.

Let's try an example:

Q. *Why* do you have a career in sales?

A. I worked in sales with my dad's business when I was young and enjoyed it.

Q. *Why?*

A. Because I always liked meeting new people and having a chance to sell something to someone.

Q. *Why?*

A. It was exciting to make a sales commission and to realize I could make as much money as I wanted.

Q. *Why?*

A. Because then I could get better and better at sales and live a more exciting life.

Q. *Why?*

A. So I don't get bored, since I know if I'm not constantly doing things, I get depressed.

Can you see how this could keep going? No telling where you might wind up!

Let's dig deeper. Notice that the answer to the second *Why* provided two sources of enjoyment: people and sales. With the third question *Why?* the answer took the path of money (and not people) and from there went to wealth and back to personal introspection.

Do you find any pattern to your answers when you do this with yourself? Do your answers seem to dive to deeper levels of purpose or reason each time you express them? *Which* personal values seem to emerge from your answers? *Which* reasons appear to feel right with your personal values. *Which* answers might you challenge as being either shallow or perhaps even silly?

Did you gain any insight about what drives you? Is there any connection to the values you hold most important?

Try this experiment again. This time choose a different subject. Begin asking yourself *why* about this subject, then repeat asking *why* to every answer you give.

Examine the answers that came up as you asked the question *Why* for the third, fourth, or fifth time. Are there any

Why

- Becaus I liwe sleep + marry + thingood Air

- Because I'm good List + I have insy ideas

- Because I realy cane abft thir Happisue

- Because I want Them to Be happy + suc so no can havenhadpsoc

- So There is less poverty misery + strugge

- Because humans do sema peoutufet wle

we Shd send
d 1,000 @
to Donaldson

similarities to the answers you came up with during the same exercise applied to a different subject matter? Do you find any consistencies? If so, these subjects may represent your underlying values or beliefs that continue to drive your actions.

The ultimate question is "Why does your business exist?" An even tougher question is "Why do I exist?"

*We are here on earth to do good for others.*
*What the others are here for, I don't know.*
—W. H. Auden

## Case History: A Personal Story of *Which* and *Why*

While I was pursuing my mechanical engineering degree at Rutgers University, I worked for several engineering firms. I received great feedback from my employers about my engineering talent.

Yet something was still not right for me. I knew in my heart I was not as happy as I really wanted to be. There was something inside that had to come out. I intuitively knew my greatest contribution would not necessarily be in my chosen field.

This seemed confusing to me. If I was doing something I was good at—or even enjoyed—what in the world could be missing? Great learning was about to take place.

One evening I sat down and asked myself some tough questions. Why was I getting my degree in engineering? What had led me to that decision? Was it where I wanted to be?

On the surface, I came up with the obvious answers. I was good at engineering and enjoyed it as well. What other criteria were important to me? Deep inside was a sense of knowing, a truth that was tougher to acknowledge to myself out loud.

Guess who else had an engineering background in my family. Yes. That was easy for you, wasn't it? My father was a great mechanic and electrician, able to fix anything. My older brother had pursued an electrical engineering degree and my cousin was studying to become a mechanical engineer as well. Becoming an engineer would certainly fit with my family's profile. But, as you know, choosing a career path because it is "in your genes" is not necessarily the best reason.

After coming to this realization, I was faced squarely with the question of choice. *Which* career should I pursue?

To address this question I began to take notice of little things that occurred on the job. *Which* moments were creating the most joy in my life? Were they moments when I truly felt I "knew my stuff" as an engineer? Or were they moments of curiosity and excitement to be learning something new?

I found that my greatest moments of joy were not necessarily in being a great engineer, but instead, in being engaged with other engineers in discussing business opportunities and dealing with the people issues common to every organization. Yet I knew little about business or human resources. It just seemed so intriguing. I learned more about my true self by remaining in deep reflection during that week.

By the end of the week, the light bulb suddenly went on and everything seemed quite clear. As Howard Behar would say, *I found my hat!*

I decided that skill alone was an insufficient reason to pursue a career. I realized that while I could be good at many things in life, I wanted a career that held my fascination and my passion. I made the decision to pursue my master's in business administration.

When classes started at Cornell, I already had a sense that a general MBA with core courses in finance, operations, systems, marketing, and economics would not satisfy me. I wanted to learn more about organizational behavior and development, so I studied under Professors Karl Weick and Thomas Lodahl, masters in this field. That set the path I was about to take.

For the following 35 years, corporate strategy and organizational development have served as my area of specialization. In retrospect, it seems that the one question *Which* would have a profound impact on my life. Perhaps this is one of the reasons that I love to share these questions with other people. I am enamored with the power of questions.

## What Is Really Important to You?

Discovering what is truly important to you and your business is absolutely essential. It helps you answer whether you are in the right business, offering the right products or services, hiring the right people, and in general, making decisions for the right reasons.

Discovering what is important can also make you more conscious of the reasons your business decides to pursue certain opportunities. Determining how to incorporate these values into decision criteria will help ground your business in what is most important.

For example, I have clients whose criteria include whether a decision improves revenues, profits, net worth, market share, brand equity, competitive position, customer satisfaction, employee satisfaction, or community standing. These are examples of worthy criteria, yet your own criteria should reflect what is important within *your* business. Some of my clients cite additional criteria as bold as having fun, whether they enjoy being with specific clients, or even whether their customers share their personal values.

Here's an additional question: Do the values your company expresses truly drive your business? I would encourage you to read *Walk the Talk, and Get the Results You Want* by Eric Harvey and Alexander Lucia. It's an eye-opener. Do your executives "walk the talk"? Are your company's values really being carried out?

Abraham Maslow gave us a gift in his "Hierarchy of Needs" to help us think about what is important. It is difficult to achieve self-actualization (the need listed at the top of his hierarchy pyramid) if we are deprived of food and shelter (the most basic of needs).

As you examine your own situation, identify which levels of need you have. Is there a hierarchy to your personal values? *Which* values do you hold most sacred?

> *Nothing is more important than connecting with your **purpose**. Nothing is as rich. Nothing is more real.*
> —Deepak Chopra

Become conscious of your personal values and when you bring those values into the business decisions you make. Do you include what is important to your employees in your list of business decision criteria? Are you content with your current knowledge, or are you always on a quest to learn new things? Do you have a desire to give something back to your community? What reasons drive your business decisions other than the obvious ones that may come off your financial statement?

## The Decision Matrix: Which Versus Why

Creating a decision matrix like the sample chart that follows is helpful to fully think through why you are making the choices you make. This is particularly helpful to a group of people who need to build consensus on a major choice they are about to make.

Across the top of the page, list in columns the various alternatives you are considering for a given subject. These potential strategies come from the question *which.*

Down the left side of the page, list the criteria you will consider to help you decide which opportunity to pursue. These come from addressing the question *why.* The sample chart lists potential criteria within certain categories (e.g., strategic, economic). The list you create should relate to your own criteria, no matter the format or whether you use any weighting system.

Evaluate each alternative strategy using a scale of 1 to 5 (with 5 being the highest score), or use a score of A-B-C, or any other means you choose, including just marking an X when criteria are met.

*Which* of your alternative strategies received the highest scores? Lowest scores? What conclusions did you come to? Are you offering certain products or services for the reasons you thought?

Does it appear that certain criteria are far more important than others? Should all criteria be given equal weight in your decision, or should certain criteria be weighted more heavily than others? Should some criteria be deleted from your list, or other new criteria added?

What answers to the question *Why* would others on your team give? *Which* criteria would your board of directors (or closest advisors) use? *Which* of the criteria you listed are universal factors, and *which* criteria are specific to the subject you are evaluating?

## Sample Decision Matrix

The chart on the next page is an illustration prepared by one company of the various factors it considered in evaluating

# SAMPLE DECISION MATRIX
Evaluate Opportunities (Which?) Against Decision Criteria (Why?)

| | | NEW OPPORTUNITY | | |
|---|---|:---:|:---:|:---:|
| SCALE: 5= Highest Value 1 = Lowest Value | | **A** | **B** | **Comments** |
| **STRATEGIC VALUE** | | | | |
| Supports long-term vision | | | | |
| Builds strategic equity value for future acquisition or IPO | | | | |
| Differentiates us from our competitors and builds intellectual capital | | | | |
| Builds greater barriers to entry for new competitors | | | | |
| Opens new markets for growth | | | | |
| **Average Rating** | | | | |
| **ECONOMIC VALUE** | | | | |
| Potential of securing investment capital or debt for funding | | | | |
| Effect on revenue stream within next five years | | | | |
| Effect on net earnings within next five years | | | | |
| Ability of leveraging to other new opportunities | | | | |
| **Average Rating** | | | | |
| **CUSTOMER VALUE** | | | | |
| Responds to needs of major customers | | | | |
| Generates new customers or promotes more business with existing customers | | | | |
| Strengthens existing customer relationships and loyalty | | | | |
| Demonstrates our commitment to innovation | | | | |
| Avoids conflict or competition with existing customers | | | | |
| **Average Rating** | | | | |
| **CULTURE VALUE** | | | | |
| Fosters the interests of key management and future leadership | | | | |
| Supports our values and guiding principles | | | | |
| Fosters our mission and value proposition | | | | |
| Fosters employee interest and excitement | | | | |
| Utilizes our core knowledge, skills and resources | | | | |
| **Average Rating** | | | | |
| **RISK MANAGEMENT VALUE** | | | | |
| Initiative can be pursued within acceptable quality standards | | | | |
| Minimizes financial, operational, and cultural risk or harm to us | | | | |
| Engages senior management within a suitable timeframe and fit with other priorities | | | | |
| Avoids substantial dilution of executive and senior management time | | | | |
| Utilizes existing resources, systems and infrastructure without conflict | | | | |
| **Average Rating** | | | | |
| AVERAGE RATING FOR ALL FACTORS COMBINED | | | | |

growth opportunities: strategic, economic, customer, culture, and operational values.

How you use such a matrix depends on your particular situation. Among a few of my engineering and manufacturing clients, executives use a weighting system that allows certain factors to be counted as more important than others, depending on the subjects being evaluated.

Other companies use the group scores as a series of "gates." If there is insufficient economic value, for example, the project is not analyzed further. Still other companies seek strategic opportunities to increase their market share and place less emphasis on shorter-term revenue gains.

The key is to use whatever criteria make sense in your situation so you have a valid basis for drawing conclusions.

## Applications of the Decision Matrix

This fundamental tool that combines *Which* and *Why* has been used by my clients for the following types of decisions:

- Evaluation of U.S. retail distribution outlets by diamond manufacturers in India and China
- Evaluation of espresso machine distribution channels, roasters, and retailers
- Evaluation of business and consumer market segments by a multimedia marketing/print company
- Evaluation of geographic expansion opportunities by a commercial real estate firm
- Evaluation of competitive technologies within the GPS industry
- Evaluation of aerospace market opportunities for a distribute-to-print information provider
- Evaluation of distribution channels for a software company in the "smart phone" industry

*The art of leadership is to say no, not yes.*
*It is very easy to say yes.*
—Tony Blair

## Case History: *Which* versus *Why*

An engineering firm specialized in seven major international markets. The board of directors asked the CEO to evaluate all markets with the criteria the board established. When the ranking was complete, only three of the seven businesses passed the threshold of a reasonably attractive score.

The board made the tough decision for the firm to pursue *only* the three business segments with high value and gradually disengaged from the other four segments. It was tough to say no to business, yet as a consequence, the firm's global reputation for specialization improved and its business continues to flourish.

The board's answers to the question *Why* gave rise to a common strategy of depth versus breadth. Years later the CEO said to me, "Before, we were an inch deep and a mile wide; today we are focused on just a few things we do incredibly well, and it sure has paid off."

Ask most CEOs whether it is easier to say yes or no and they will respond with *yes*. In a normal desire to grab more customers, offer more services, and "be all that we can be," we tend to say yes and broaden our business too quickly. Being able to say no for the right reasons helps us stay focused. A strong leader knows when to say no.

Becoming conscious of *why* we make the business decisions we make can help uncover new and exciting opportunities, or help eliminate products or services we offer that are not creating the results we want. In essence, examining the question *Why* and using our answers as decision criteria can help grow our business in a manner consistent with the values we hold. Thus, your answers to the question *Why* help you understand the rationale behind your answers to the other six of the seven questions.

Continually using the question *Why* helps ensure that daily actions match your strategic intent. The question *Why* will cause top-of-mind awareness of your mission. Because your mission should link to all other actions in the company, it is one of the most important statements you can make (along with values, vision, and goals).

> *Mission statement work is the single most important work because the decisions made there affect all other decisions.*
> —Dr. Stephen R. Covey
> *The 7 Habits of Highly Effective People*

## What Is Your Mission?

These days many companies are crafting mission statements and posting them for the world to see. This would seem to be "the American thing to do" because customers are intrigued with how we view our grand purpose. Yet many consumers regard these statements as "mush." Some statements make you want to put your hand to your heart as if saluting the American flag. Other statements bring up warm memories of mom and apple pie.

The only real question is whether your mission statement is adding any *value*. Do customers want to do business with you because of it? Do employees want to perform better because of it? Do investors want to give you money because of it? These questions are important to ask for all constituencies of your business—suppliers, alliances, and the general public.

Most businesses form their mission without ever asking their customers what they think. Many mission statements are simply an *identity statement* describing what service or product is being offered. Such mission statements are boring because they state the obvious. Don't fall into that trap. Create a mission that has passion!

A mission statement should describe the ultimate value a company's product or service provides to its customer or client and thus should directly address the *Why* behind the business. Whether presented in a short or long format, the mission should describe the *value* received—the *result* of providing the product or service.

Your answers to the question *Why* reveal the purpose underlying the ultimate value of your product or service. Many companies consider this their mission.

> *When you discover your **mission**, you will feel its demand. It will fill you with enthusiasm and a burning desire to get to work on it.*
> —W. Clement Stone

### Case History: Physio-Control

Physio-Control, a division of Medtronic, is a Seattle manufacturer of defibrillators used by medics for patients with heart failure. Many years ago its executives gave me a desktop plaque that reads "Our mission is to save lives."

This is followed by the inscription "We do this by providing unique medical devices of the highest quality, which predict or urgently intervene in life-threatening, cardiorespiratory events."

Physio-Control later changed its mission to "Lifesaving equipment for lifesaving teams." A tagline reads "Lifesaving Starts Here."

I present two alternative mission statements for the same company to give you an opportunity to improve your skills by considering some standard questions:

- Who is the audience for each statement?
- What is the value delivered to each audience?
- Which statement do you respond to better if you are the: employee, purchasing agent, medic, patient?
- Which statement is the more enduring?
- Which statement is easier to pronounce?
- Which statement is more memorable?
- Which statement is better for sales?
- Which statement is better for employee productivity?
- Which statement is better for customer relations?
- Which statement is more appealing to the community?
- Which statement is more appealing to investors?
- Which statement is more appealing to you?

Now apply these same considerations to your own mission statement. What conclusions do you reach? How can your mission have a greater long-term impact and create the response you intend?

## Examples of Mission Statements

I often use the The Walt Disney Company as an example because everyone is familiar with it. When I ask audiences what Disney's mission is, most people come up with some expression of fun. The entrance to Disney has a sign: Happiest Place on Earth. Notice it is not a long paragraph, nor does it speak of the rides you will go on. The statement is singular in theme, short, easy to pronounce, and memorable.

Disney's statement works because it is customer-driven. It is the *value* Disney delivers to its customers, in the form of a feeling.

The following are examples of mission statements that identify the value the business delivers to its customers. (My observation notes list the products or services not mentioned even as the mission remains a strong statement.)

- Washington Athletic Club: "To enrich the quality of life of our members." *(Observe this does not mention athletics, hotel, or restaurants.)*
- Business Interiors Northwest: "Delivering spaces that inspire" *(Observe this does not mention furniture.)*
- Kibble & Prentice: "Building net worth and managing risks." *(Observe this does not mention insurance or investments.)*
- AEI Music: "To influence the way consumers shop, buy and dine." *(Observe this does not mention music.)*
- AAA Washington: "To provide safe and satisfying travel experiences better than our members can arrange on their own." *(Observe this does not mention autos.)*
- CourtLink: "Making access to court records easier." *(Observe this does not mention software.)*
- Space Needle: "To provide every guest with an unforgettable experience that surpasses their expectation." *(Observe this does not mention the facility.)*
- Voyager Capital: "To promote innovation and remove barriers to help people realize their dreams." *(Observe this does not mention funding.)*

## Factors to Consider in Preparing Your Mission

Most mission statements begin with an action verb and then state the value received. Good mission statements have the ability to be used in everyday language, beginning with "Our mission is to _____."

The best mission statements have the following six characteristics:

- *Memorable*—Express a compelling singular theme succinctly (may also have a long version that follows the short expression)
- *Customer-Oriented*—State the ultimate value that results for the customer
- *Credible*—Reflect reality; are true to the company's position in the marketplace
- *Aligned*—Are linked with other strategic intent statements, such as vision, values, and goals
- *Applicable*—Are usable in a variety of media applications and presentations
- *Pronounceable*—Are easily spoken and enunciated; avoid complex expressions

## Critique Your Own Mission Statement

When I meet with an executive team, I often ask the question, "What is *your* mission?" I pay attention to how quickly anyone responds with the same answer (which is rare). Sometimes there are various versions expressed.

Sometimes an executive begins poring through files to find the page. At other times someone leaves the room and comes back with a plaque from the lobby. Unfortunately, these are all signs of a mission statement that is having little or no effect.

Unless your mission statement directly reflects the value you are proposing to your customer in doing business with you, and does so in a way that is easily remembered and acted on, it may not be providing the value you intended.

If you find yourself stumped to come up with your own answer, simply ask your major customers, "*Why* do you do business with us?" Your customers will reveal your mission to you.

## Values Statements

In addressing the subject of mission, you were asked to identify the *Why,* or underlying purpose, of your product or service from your customer's perspective. Let's also apply the question *Why* more broadly to your business and address why you are in this particular business. Which values are most important to you and *why?*

Many companies have their most important values expressed in a *values statement.* Values are the principles and beliefs we hold to be sacred. Values express what is most important to an organization or person.

### Examples of Values

- Washington Athletic Club: "leadership, excellence, integrity, service, and sensitivity"
- Business Interiors Northwest: "expertise, personal integrity, company unity, customer value, community contribution, service, and continuous learning."
- UNICO Properties LLC: "tenant and client satisfaction, employee satisfaction and challenge, financial performance"
- Diversified Industrial Services: "We value all people; we embrace excellence; we advocate community inclusion."
- U.S. Army: "loyalty, duty, respect, selfless service, honor, integrity, personal courage." (Note: The U.S. Army is not a client of mine.)

The values expressed by your business are important, though what is more important is whether your business actually lives up to them.

## An Opportunity to Build Inclusion

Company values concern everyone connected with the company. Therefore, the process for clarifying company values can, and should, involve any employee at any level—in contrast to company *vision*, which is expected to be developed by the CEO, the senior executive team, and the board of directors.

Company cultures that encourage the sharing of stories of achieving incredible customer loyalty often revolve around some important principle, or value, that is rooted in the answers to the question *Why*.

The question *Why* is one of the most powerful questions among The Seven Questions because it has several unique qualities:

- It addresses the purpose, motive, cause, or rationale underlying decisions, whether conscious or unconscious.
- It implies a future state of being, result, or effect achieved or desired.
- It explains answers to the other six questions by combining with them in a matrix format, such as a decision matrix of *Which* versus *Why*.
- It helps all parties understand the big picture of intention.

## Key Lessons of This Chapter

1. The question *Why* addresses the purpose, motives, reasons, and ultimate value your business delivers to all constituents.
2. The values you determine to be most important are what should be used frequently in guiding your decisions.

3. An effective mission does *not* describe what you do; it describes the *value* of what you do from your customer's perspective.

## Actions to Take

1. Create a memorable mission statement that conveys the value of your business to the marketplace. This will help you sell your ideas to others.
2. Test your mission with trusted friends, family and customers. Listen to their feedback.
3. Decide how you can implement your mission and demonstrate you are serious about it by taking action.

## Building Your Progress

You have now addressed the two key questions for your business:

1. You have reexamined your niche and alternative **choices** and have gained new insight into *which* business to be in, which market to target, which products and services to sell, and through which distribution channels to sell them.
2. You have examined *why* you are in this business and the **purpose** and motives behind your thinking, and have clarified the key decision criteria you will use in making your most important decisions.

These last two chapters served to help you identify the right choices for your business and to make these choices for the right reasons. The significant questions "*Which* business are you really in and *why*?" demonstrate how answering just two of *The Seven Questions* can influence your business.

Take a pit stop to refresh before moving on. Then take your strategy journal out of your desk drawer, or open up that digital file, and take advantage of this moment by writing down your notes.

What are the most significant conclusions you came to about your business as a result of getting through the chapters on *Which* and *Why?* Can you list a few major business challenges you face, for which clear answers to *Which* and *Why* will help grow your business? If so, great!

By gradually bringing clarity to your answers to The Seven Questions, your intention will be more focused and the results you achieve will improve.

The next Chapter, *Where*, addresses the direction in which you and your industry are moving. A clear and compelling company vision can make a difference. Interested? Read on.

# CHAPTER 4: WHERE?
## The Element of Position

*The world makes a path for the man
who knows **where** he is going.*
—Ralph Waldo Emerson

## The Essence of *Where* Conveys Position

The question *Where* conveys the current or future position of some thing or person in the context of its surroundings. *"Where are we?"* is a question of current position, usually in the context of geography, but it can be in relation to any dimension or situation.

A future position implies a sense of direction and intended movement. *"Where* are we headed?" can be answered as a general direction (e.g., north) or as a specific destination or position (e.g., two miles south). The answer to *"Where* are we headed?" may also be expressed as a broad change of circumstance or eventual state of being (e.g., *"Where* everyone has clean drinking water"). Thus, the essence of *Where* may be a direction, destination, position, or situation of the future in relation to the present.

## Location-Based Services

Last year I had the pleasure of serving as the interim CEO of Loctronix Corporation, for which I serve on its board of directors. Loctronix's scientists and engineers have recently been awarded patents on Spectral Compression Positioning, a new technology that locates people or assets in any environment—indoors, outdoors, or underground. The mission of Loctronix is "to locate anyone or anything, everywhere."

Michael B. Mathews, Ph.D., Loctronix's founder and president, said, "Universal positioning will become a fundamental utility. This will let us know **where** anything or anyone is at all times, ultimately having a profound impact on how our information technology interacts with us."

As an example, the recent introduction of Google Latitude enables users to locate friends and family with cell phones. This application uses GPS plus Wi-Fi and cell towers to supplement coverage. GPS is limited, however, because it does not work well in downtown corridors, indoors, or underground, so greater accuracy of information will be needed in the future (and help is on the way).

The fundamental utility of location technology—the utility of where—is driving tremendous growth in the location-based services industry. The world market for location services exceeds $22 billion today, and some analysts predict that it will exceed $200 billion by 2020.

As humans, we all have an instinctive desire to know *where* we are positioned in relation to our surroundings, or to know *where* someone or something else is in relation to ourselves. Similarly, as entrepreneurs, executives, investors, or customers, we have this same desire to know where a business is in relation to its competitors.

The following section illustrates one such approach.

## Competitive Positioning

Consider for a moment a major customer you currently have. Why did that customer purchase your service or product? What were their major considerations? Was their decision based on your company's reputation, skill, service, price, location, history, trust, who referred them to you, just your good looks, or some other factor?

The list could go on and on. Take a moment and decide for yourself what *you* feel are the most important factors. Now do the same exercise again from your *customer's* point of view. For which factors might there be a difference of viewpoint between how the market sees your business versus your own viewpoint?

If you were to consider *where* your business is positioned in relation to your major competitors, how would you draw a picture of this? A fairly common approach is to select the two most important factors, such as price and quality, and use these as the two dimensions of a map. Then place the logos of your business and your competitors on the map. (See next page.)

If you want to create a picture that illustrates more than two factors your market considers in buying your products or services, the Competitive Positioning chart shows an easy way to visualize where your business is positioned in relation to your competitors.

My pet name for this format is the "graphic equalizer chart" because it reminds me of stereo equipment used to adjust various frequencies. If this is not your thing and you are hungry at the moment, the chart might look more like skewers on a barbecue.

Whatever image comes to your mind, remember it vividly. Strategies to increase the value to your customer often present new business opportunities.

Try sketching your own chart for your business. What would you select as the most important purchase factors and where would you rate your business and that of your major competitors?

Once you have done this, identify where you would like to reposition your business in the future. Where would you move players to show the most probable future position of each business? This difference in positioning over time represents a strategic chess board. Will existing players fall off the board? Will new players enter the board?

On the chart shown, higher marks vertically for quality, service, reputation, and guarantee represent high value to the buyer. The dimension of price, however, can be viewed as the opposite, or else it needs to be defined.

If price is viewed purely as the price of the product or service, then a high mark indicates high price, which does not

## COMPETITIVE POSITIONING
### The Market Differentiates Your Company
### Based on Their Criteria

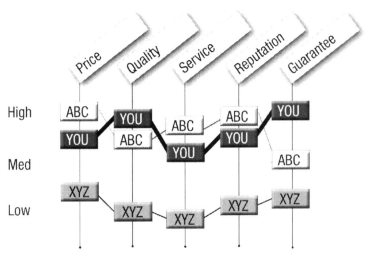

© Copyright 2009 Strategic Development Corporation

necessarily indicate greater value to the buyer. In that case, you wouldn't necessarily want to have a higher mark than your competitors.

If, however, you want all high marks on the chart to be interpreted as better value for the buyer, then you can define price to mean "price value"—economic value to the purchaser in relation to what is received. This would mean that a higher position on the chart would represent higher value to the buyer.

If the fictitious example shown were actually the case, the firm being illustrated would appear to have developed a superior product compared with its competitors. It offers a superior guarantee, although service levels could be bolstered further to be more competitive.

What would be your strategy to strengthen this position? What would your strategy be if you were the competitor? Can you envision how you might want to adjust your future positioning?

Now let's get back to the reality of the sketch you drew for *your* business. What preliminary conclusions can you make about your competitive positioning? What additional information would you need to make your evaluation more meaningful? Would your customers rate you differently than you rated yourself?

Consider whether there is value in having a more in-depth analysis of your business and market. If so, decide *who* should complete the chart. For your first draft, try doing this yourself based on your own intuition of the market.

Some of my clients have their sales team complete the charts for their strategic business units. Others engage their marketing department to conduct a direct customer survey, or include noncustomers. Still others engage professional market research firms and marketing consultants to help in the evaluation. Choose the resource that best fits your situation and your need for valid market information.

## The Direction of Your Industry

Apply the concept of positioning to your business. *Where* is your business heading in relation to products, services, markets, competitors, and the entire industry?

What major changes in direction has your business taken in the last several years? Did these shifts eventually achieve the desired result?

Have you kept, and do you continue to keep, your management team, customers, board, and investors aware of the position of your business and your competitors?

## Force Field Analysis

In considering *where* your business is now and *where* it is headed, it is helpful to identify *all* of the forces that affect your business and industry.

External forces may include local, national, or global economies, regulation, legislation, consumer trends, technology trends, and environmental trends.

There are also internal forces influencing the direction of your business. These forces may include executive leadership, business infrastructure, marketing, branding, research, product development, and strategic alliances.

Each force can be displayed as a vector with its own magnitude and direction, exerting an influence on the position of your business.

*Where* your particular business is headed is the sum of the magnitude and direction of all forces combined. The overall direction represents the sum of all forces, each having its own momentum of mass times velocity.

## FORCE FIELD ANALYSIS
### Evaluate Forces Impacting Your Business

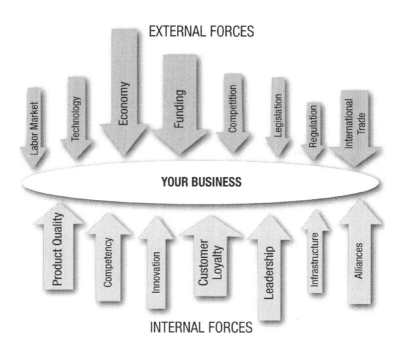

© Copyright 2009 Strategic Development Corporation

Here are some questions to consider in drawing the forces that affect your business:

1. Which *external* forces are currently affecting your business most? Will these forces be more or less intense during the next five to ten years?
2. Which *internal* forces can you apply to your advantage? Which areas need to be strengthened?
3. What is the *net effect* of all forces on your business and how does this affect your strategy?

4.  What is the most significant strategic *initiative* you could embark on to exert forces in the direction you intend?

Consider new external forces that may affect your business, such as the credit crisis, new regulations, international trade, price of oil, global warming, or the threat of terrorism. Also consider how internal forces may be changing, such as how generational demographics—from baby boomers to Gen X to millennials—are influencing human resource practices.

It is evident that our future will be dissimilar from the past. As a result, we must continually confront whether we are making correct assumptions, such as the availability of capital to grow, restrictions of any form in doing business with certain market segments, and other significant concerns.

### Case History: Seafirst Bank

In 1982 Seafirst was the major regional bank in the Pacific Northwest. I was hired as vice president and manager of Corporate Strategy, with a specific charter to take advantage of pending interstate banking deregulation.

At the time, Seafirst began forming a consortium of West Coast banks to compete with First Interstate Bank. Code-named "Westnet", the consortium was being led by Seafirst and included Wells Fargo in California, Valley National Bank in Phoenix, U.S. Bancorp in Portland, United Bank of Colorado in Denver, and Bancorp Hawaii.

We were conducting special projects, such as deployment of regional lock boxes, knowing that major industry forces would be changing the competitive landscape. Our entire department focused on understanding major external forces and developing corresponding business growth strategies.

Unfortunately for Seafirst, another major internal force brewing at the same time was not being managed well and eventually caused Seafirst to abandon its Westnet pre-merger strategy. This devastating force, dubbed the Synergies of Size Initiative, was created by an executive mandate to grow bank assets rapidly. The bank did grow rapidly but also undertook risks with insufficient attention to loan quality. Ultimately, major loans in the oil industry defaulted and caused Seafirst to be acquired by Bank of America.

I left Seafirst in January 1983 before it was acquired, and I founded Strategic Development Corporation, a management consulting practice specializing in business growth strategies. Armed with my favorite tool—The Seven Questions—and what I learned at Seafirst (critical issues management), I began helping companies that were undergoing major transitions. I also realized that the decision matrix of *Which* and *Why*, which I have often used for targeting growth opportunities, could be suddenly rendered irrelevant if trumped by a major force that influenced *where* the industry was headed.

## The Direction of the Future

The question *Where?* conveys a direction of the future. The duration of the future being considered is directly related to the "altitude" at which the vision is being sought. At ground level, the future may be seen in tactical steps to achieve the next objective. At 40,000 feet, the future may be conceived as broader, strategic changes.

*Where* are the major forces at play headed? How do these forces interact with one another? What is the culminating effect on your business? How can your business take advantage of these forces? How will your industry change as a result of these forces? Continue to think of other questions in relation to *where* your business is being positioned in order to build a comprehensive view of how the business climate will change.

As you "step back and step up," your perspective begins to get broader, enabling you to view your situation from a better vantage point. The additional insight you gain can be significant. As the familiar analogy goes, a good manager guides his team through the trees; a good leader climbs a tree to ensure the team is in the right forest.

Devoting time to contemplating *where* your business is headed is as worthwhile as completing short-term actions. Business health, as well as personal health, is a question of balance. For this reason, devote sufficient time in your business to contemplate the future.

You and your business exist in a river of forces. How do these forces come into existence? Economists have argued for centuries about how forces such as the global economy get created. The more important question is how you, or your business, can create your own internal forces. The momentum you create as a business leader by solidifying your mission, vision, and values can become a major force to your advantage.

## THE RESULTS YOU ACHIEVE
## DEPEND ON YOUR CLARITY.

### Strategic Intent

*Where* would you prefer your business head? What would you want your business to *be* in the future? Your response to these important questions can be expressed as a *vision statement*. Your vision statement should reflect a future state of being you want to achieve. What is the relationship between your vision and mission?

Strategic intent represents the most important statements of intention by a business, including mission, values, vision, goals, and strategies.

The following chart lists the five major components of strategic intent. What a company holds as most sacred, its values, serve to guide development of mission and vision. Goals create the metrics that gauge success in achieving a vision, and strategies are the broad approaches by which goals will be achieved.

## STRATEGIC INTENT
### The Most Important Statements of Intention

© Copyright 2009 Strategic Development Corporation

## Vision Statements

A vision statement addresses the question of *where* a business is headed. The difference between mission and vision is that a mission statement describes *doing* something to achieve an intended result; a vision statement describes a future state of *being*.

> *First say to yourself what you would **be**;*
> *and then do what you have to **do**.*
> —Epictetus

Vision statements fall into two categories: (1) *relative* vision statements, and (2) *absolute* vision statements.

A relative vision statement describes a future state of market positioning in relation to the competition. Most companies have relative vision statements. These statements most often begin with the verb phrase *to be,* as in "To be _____." In short, vision statements describe a general direction of company positioning in specific terms.

Absolute vision statements are not formulated in relation to the competition, but instead convey an ideal state of being, or result of providing a product or service—whether or not the statement ever comes true.

Let's look at examples of each category.

## Examples of Relative Vision Statements

- Business Interiors Northwest: "To be the leading provider of commercial furniture and services in the Northwest"
- Washington Athletic Club: "To be the premier athletic club in America"
- Cinnabon: "To be the dominant specialty bakery retailer"
- Space Needle: "To be recognized as the Northwest's premier special occasion facility"
- Kibble & Prentice: "To be the trusted solution for insurance, qualified plan administration, and investment services"
- CourtLink: "To be the dominant provider of electronic access to our nation's court records"
- AEI Music: "To be The Source of custom music and imaging for retail, worldwide"
- Disney: "To be the No. 1 resort destination in the world"

- Snapple: "To be #3."
- Hand & Stone Massage Spa: "To be the premier spa in the State of Washington."

### Examples of Absolute (nonrelative) Vision Statements

- Physio-Control: "We envision a society in which no person dies suddenly as a result of a cardiorespiratory event."
- Coca-Cola: "To have a Coke in arm's reach of everyone on the planet"

## Short and Long Format Statements

Your mission, vision, and values can be expressed in both short and long formats.

Short-form statements serve the purpose of being memorable, such as Disney's mission "Happiest place on earth" and vision "To be the No. 1 resort destination in the world."

There are times when more in-depth statements of mission and vision are needed. Your customers may want to know what your mission or vision mean to them.

Suppose your mission focused on innovation and creativity. Would this mean your customers expect your firm to provide leading-edge technologies? If your vision is to be a market leader, would this mean your customers will experience lower or higher pricing for your services?

For your customers, express what your mission and vision really mean to them. This will enable your sales team to create more powerful presentations about your mission and vision.

Consider what your mission and vision mean to your employees. If your intention is to be the very best in your industry, does achieving this vision mean you will hire only the very best talent? Does this translate to compensation practices that call for above-market salaries or incentive programs?

Each constituency wants to understand the implications for them. This understanding allows you to create additional statements that might follow your short-form mission or vision. Consider preparing both formats so you can use either format depending on your audience and situation.

## Factors to Consider in Crafting Your Vision

Which factors are relevant in crafting your vision statement? As a prelude to your discussions on vision with your team members, consider these questions:

*Where* are we headed in relation to our...

- product or service offering?
- competitive position?
- systems infrastructure?
- marketplace?
- brand evolution?
- customers?
- technology?

What other dimensions should you consider in addressing *where* your business is headed? Write them down here or in your journal.

## Key Lessons of This Chapter

1. The question *Where* directly conveys position or movement of position. Fundamental to effective strategic positioning and business growth are knowing *where* your business stands today and *where* you intend it to be in the future.

2. Articulate *where* your industry stands today and where it is headed. Identify the forces that will shape your

industry and determine how these will affect your future.

3. The question *Where* conveys direction. As the driver of your business, you are responsible for the direction your organization is headed. *Where* are you driving to? State your vision in clear, memorable terms.

## Actions to Take

1. Create your own competitive positioning chart, depicting where you are in relation to your competitors.

2. Ensure the chart is "real" from the perspective of the marketplace. Consider feedback from not only your key customers, but also from prospective customers that elect to use your competitor instead.

3. Based on your answers, do you want to maintain or change your position in relation to your competitors?

## You are Making Progress on Strategic Thinking

You have now addressed three of the key strategic questions for your business:

1. You have reexamined your niche and alternative **choices** and have gained new insight into *which* business to be in, which market to target, which products and services to sell, and through which distribution channels to sell them.

2. You have examined *why* you are in this business and the **purpose** and motives behind your thinking, and have clarified the key decision criteria you will use in making your most important decisions.

3. You have explored *where* your industry is headed, where your business is headed, and where you want your future market **position** and vision to be.

## Your Next Step Is Addressing *Who?*

Take a moment and clarify, in your own mind, where you want your business to go. *Write this down in your strategy journal or right here:*




Now begin to consider the people in your business. Can you imagine them in your vision of where your business is headed? As leaders, how will they shape the culture and brand of your company?

You know deep inside that your success will depend on having the right people. Fortunately, that's the subject of the next chapter, Who.

# CHAPTER 5: WHO?
## The Element of People

*Wearing one hat is the epitome of leadership. It is the starting point — and the end point — of the lifelong process of discovering who you are and what you stand for.*
    —Howard Behar
        *It's Not About the Coffee*

## The Essence of *Who* Conveys People

The question *Who* reflects the subject of people. As it applies to your business, the question *"Who* are we?" can be applied to individual executives as leaders who drive the business, or more broadly as the entire group of employees representing your company, such as "Who are we in the marketplace?" The latter is more of a branding and market positioning question; the former is more a question of leadership. Both considerations are worth exploring.

Is the question *Who?* strategic or operational? The answer is really both, depending on how the question is applied.

As you recall from the Introduction, The Seven Questions serves as an interactive model whereby questions bond to each other depending on how they are used. *Who* are we as a company is a strategic matter, as it pertains to market positioning and branding. Internally, the subject of people and *who* is responsible is an organizational matter. Rather than splitting hairs, this chapter is devoted to broad aspects of the question *Who.*

## It's All About People

My experience consulting with a multitude of businesses has given me a strong perspective on issues that have a great impact on business success. From my view, the single most important element for success is leadership.

I have observed businesses that have an outstanding value proposition with enormous potential, yet they achieve only mediocre results. Why? In these businesses, I find an energetic founder who simply has not had success in selecting the right talent to join his or her venture. It may be comfortable at first to turn to those we know for support and ask them to join our business, rather than seek the best talent for the position. This is a mistake.

The converse is also true. I'll come across an outstanding leader whom others will follow anywhere. Even for businesses encumbered with substantial challenges, if the right people are on board, they will find a way to solve the problems.

There is substantial truth in the notion that outstanding leaders will create outstanding businesses.

> *When the Master governs, the people are hardly aware that he exists. Next best is the leader who is loved. Next, the one who is feared. The worst is one who is despised. The Master doesn't talk, he acts. When his work is done, the people say, "Amazing, we did it, all by ourselves!"*
>
> —Lau-tzu
> *Tao te Ching*
> (Translation by Stephen Mitchell)

### Case History: Leadership Transition

Many years ago I was engaged as strategy counsel to a large engineering and manufacturing firm. After we had conducted strategic planning in all five divisions of the company, the chairman called me to his office to discuss the status of the engagement. He wanted to know the relationship between critical issues and strategic planning.

I asked him what he believed was the most critical issue facing his company. He told me the board's critical issue was determining who would succeed him as CEO. He had contemplated selecting the vice president of research and development as the next CEO.

I asked why. He told me this person was an outstanding electrical engineer (the chairman himself was also an engineer), and for this reason he believed the VP R&D would surely succeed. I asked how the VP was perceived by other people. The chairman smiled and told me that the VP's subordinates gave him very high marks indeed.

I then asked how the other vice presidents viewed this particular candidate. The chairman shrugged. This was my clue. I asked his permission to conduct a leadership assessment. He told me to proceed even though he didn't expect to find out anything new.

In reviewing the anonymous survey results, a few of the other vice presidents said that if the VP R&D became the next CEO, they would consider resigning. Although this particular VP generated loyalty from his superior and subordinates, he had not generated enthusiasm from his peers as a team player.

Ironically, the person with the highest leadership ratings— from his boss, subordinates, peers, and frequent customer contacts as well—was the chief financial officer. This person had an extraordinary ability to understand other people and provide leadership by asking compelling questions. Everyone loved him. As a result of the board's review of his leadership ratings, he was selected as the new CEO.

During the following several years, this company's key metrics on employee satisfaction, customer satisfaction, market share, and profitability steadily improved. I have never seen a more substantial level of enthusiasm displayed by any client resulting from an organizational intervention.

One of the most significant *Who* issues currently facing baby boomer executives who own or manage a business is planning for their succession. Family-held businesses have an even more substantial challenge: Who will succeed Dad or Mom? Leadership succession is often a political and sensitive subject. From my experience, it is a question of balancing the interests of the business with the interests of the individuals.

## Progression Planning

As baby boomers age, America's business structure is facing a huge challenge: a shortage of talent to run existing businesses.

From the board rooms of large enterprises to the garages of family-held proprietorships, owners and shareholders are dealing with succession more than ever before.

During the latter half of the twentieth century, most businesses made these decisions based primarily on the needs of the company. During the last ten years, however, more businesses are paying attention to the long-term career interests of their most upwardly mobile executives and professional staff.

As the average tenure of executives with the same company has been gradually declining because of greater degrees of economic and political change, more businesses are seeking to balance the interests of their company with the interests of key individuals.

Although "succession planning" in most companies refers primarily to key leadership positions, I find that more and more companies are considering this subject as it pertains to mid-management positions as well.

Succession planning is often viewed as a secretive, political process of who will succeed whom. For this reason, I prefer to use the term *progression planning* for a more open, candid assessment of career standing.

## PROGRESSION PLANNING
### Balance the Interests of Each Stakeholder

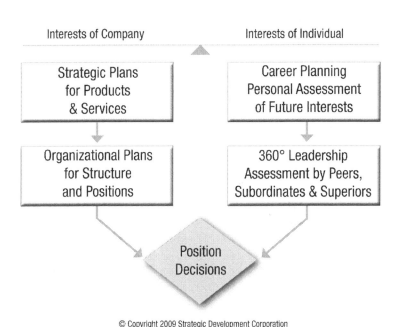

Progression planning considers how someone will progress in the organization, irrespective of occupying an executive position in the future. Some individuals want to know how to progress to a higher level of responsibility without the requirement of management responsibilities. Technically oriented individuals, for example, may want to know the requirements to become a chief scientist or engineer, purely on a technical track without having to manage other people.

The progression planning model considers the interests of the organization as well as the individual. The left side of the chart reflects the needs of your business that are driven by your strategic plan. The right side considers the career desires of the individual employee. Both of these paths must eventually merge for a decision that is in the interests of both parties.

How are the interests of both constituents balanced? The company's interests are stated by translating long-term strategic plans with specific stages of evolution of the organizational structure. This determines which positions may exist in the future, some of which may not exist today.

Such information can be matched up with an individual's assessment of his or her career interests. When individuals are provided feedback from peers, subordinates, superiors, and frequent contacts, this additional information helps them understand how they are perceived by others.

When sufficient information has been gathered on both sides of this balance equation, a solution is sought that is compelling to the individual candidates as well as to the company. The readiness of a candidate to assume a new position can be described in a variety of ways, such as:

- Ready to promote now
- Not ready yet: has sufficient knowledge, but needs more experience (more time needed in either current role or other roles that are a precursor to the position desired)
- Not ready yet: has sufficient experience, but needs more knowledge (may need training and development to acquire more knowledge necessary for the future position desired)
- Not ready for some time: needs more knowledge as well as more experience

Decisions may range from immediate action to tentative conclusions for future actions, subject to changes in future reviews and the company's changing situation.

In a progression planning model, this information is shared openly with the employee so he or she knows the requirements necessary to advance to a future position.

> *Get the right **people** on the bus, get the wrong people off the bus, and get the right people in the right seats.*
>
> —Jim Collins

## Leadership Assessment

If you undertake an assessment of your own leadership skills, or those of others, be sure to refer to the individual's ability to clearly communicate the answers to The Seven Questions.

Addressing the question *Who?* requires an objective assessment of leadership talent. What factors should you consider? The SDC (Strategic Development Corporation) Leadership Model was developed to assess a leader in four leadership quadrants, for an "all around" or "360 degree" assessment, as shown in the chart on the following page.

The four quadrants in the 360° Leadership Assessment are defined as follows:

- **Individual Leadership** – Possession of leadership character traits: integrity, passion, and influence.
- **Interpersonal Leadership** – Ability to interact effectively with employees, customers and others: promoting teamwork, creating a positive culture, and providing support.

## THE SDC LEADERSHIP MODEL
360° Leadership Assessment Instrument

© Copyright 2009 Strategic Development Corporation

- **Functional Leadership** – Mastery in one's respective functional area of expertise: being the best one can be, including being a resource to others and participating in professional development.
- **Strategic Leadership** – Ability to understand major forces that shape the industry; includes formulating vision, competitive position, and long-term strategy.

Regardless of which means of feedback you prefer to use—ranging from 360° surveys to casual feedback you get from a friend over lunch—be sure to understand for yourself the kind of leader you want to be.

Know your strengths, weaknesses, passion, and vision. Know what you stand for and what you will *not* stand for. In short, know yourself.

## Transparency and Case Histories

What are the standards of transparency in your organization? What value do you place on the behavior, attitudes, and standards of your senior leaders?

Executive behavior can have a profound impact on how an organization and its customers view the answer to "Who are we?" Listed below are a few examples I have encountered in which an executive's extreme behavior worked for, or against, the way that employees, customers, and the general marketplace viewed a company and its leadership. *(Company names have been withheld from these case examples.)*

### Positive examples of leadership's effect on culture:

- The CEO of a health care manufacturing business was known for his deep caring of people and there had been practically no employee turnover since the business was founded. Upon selling the business, the CEO and majority shareholder graciously shared half of his gain on the sale (millions of dollars) with all of the employees, based on their length of employment. He stated in a letter that it was really the hard work of dedicated employees that built the value of the company to such a high level, and they deserved it.
- A national retailer is known for its innovation. In the employee newsletter, executives discuss the mistakes they have made and what they learned. Employees do not fear taking a risk in trying something new, because of the company culture that emphasizes learning.
- A software company is progressing rapidly in its rollout and hiring employees quickly. The CEO notices that engineers and programmers are working late hours and are stressed out. He converts an executive office to a private meditation room and brings in a professional

massage therapist to give any employee free on-site massages twice a month.

**Negative examples of leadership's effect on culture:**

- A business had just finished communicating its most important values to its stakeholders, which included employee health and respect for others. Weeks later the CEO was thrown in jail for being drunk again and attacking some of the shareholders in a meeting. The board convened an emergency meeting and fired the CEO.

- A financial institution communicated its core value as appreciating and celebrating the diversity in its workforce. In an all-employee meeting, the CEO read passages from the Bible and urged religious conversion. Board members were present at the event and dismissed the CEO later that afternoon.

- An insurance firm touted one of its main values as rewarding employees for individual performance. The CEO, however, awarded the same percentage increase in salary to every employee at year-end. Employees privately complained that there was no benefit for working hard and viewed the company as a place to comfortably "retire while working," since people were neither fired nor rewarded for their performance.

> *Everyone thinks of changing the world, but no one thinks of changing himself.*
> —Leo Tolstoy

These extreme examples, positive and negative, point to the dramatic effect leaders have on their company culture and brand. You may also notice that the leader's behavior was not congruent with an intended strategy.

The chapter on *How* will provide more discussion and tools on how you can avoid these mistakes in your business and ensure that your practices are aligned with your strategies.

## The Role of the Board

Your board of directors or advisory board can be of help in setting a tone of professional leadership. The Sarbanes-Oxley Act of 2002 has had a pronounced impact on the requirement of publicly held companies to be transparent in their information. It has also raised the awareness for effective governance by directors and officers of many non-public boards.

In addition to reviewing and approving the company values, mission, vision, and goals, board members should ensure that they are upholding the values by conducting themselves in a manner commensurate with the values. For example, if the board encourages employees to be active in their community, the directors should demonstrate this by their own community support.

The National Association of Corporate Directors (NACD) has been instrumental in providing education to boards of directors around the country. If you are a director, I highly encourage you to get involved with NACD by joining your local chapter. You will be amazed at how much there is to becoming a more effective director.

Here are some questions you may want your executive team and board to address:

- How does your business ensure that your company's standards of leadership integrity and transparency are being upheld?

- When there are violations of company values that are held sacred, what actions are appropriate to guide the culture toward the standards you desire?
- In what ways do your executive team and board promote the mission, vision, and goals of your company in a visible way to your employees, customers, and community?
- What role should your board or advisory group have in developing the strategic plans of your business?
- What are the key differences in accountability between your board and executive team?

## The Authority Matrix and Case History

Many companies struggle with identifying *who* has the authority to make a decision and who will be involved in the decision. As an example, the CEO and COO of an engineering firm wanted to be clear with each other about which circumstances called for them to involve the other in decision-making.

At the time, they made most decisions jointly. But each expressed a desire to act independently of each other whenever possible. They also wanted to come to a consensus on which circumstances required a truly joint decision such that they would not act unless they agreed with each other. Finally, they recognized that for certain circumstances, although one party would be accountable for the decision, it would be important to first obtain the input from the other party before making a decision.

We constructed a chart that reflected their requests and listed the various scenarios they discussed. Each was asked to place an X in the column representing their viewpoint. The sample Authority Matrix illustrates how the CEO and COO completed the matrix.

# SAMPLE AUTHORITY MATRIX
## Identify Who Decides What for Individual versus Collaborative Responsibility

| | CEO | | Joint | COO | |
|---|:---:|:---:|:---:|:---:|:---:|
| **Authority:** Input Required: | No | Yes | Yes | Yes | No |
| **STRATEGIC** | | | | | |
| Develops vision, long-term goals, mission and values | | | X | | |
| Communicates strategic intent to employees on ongoing basis | X | | | | X |
| Oversees implementation of mission and values and assures reinforcement | | | | X | |
| Prepares Strategic Plan document | | X | | | |
| Develops strategic alliance agreements with other firms | | X | | | |
| **FINANCIAL** | | | | | |
| Oversees banking relationships and adherence to bank covenants | X | | | | |
| Oversees company investments and divestitures | X | | | | |
| Oversees development of long-term financial model | | X | | | |
| Selects management information systems | | X | | | |
| Prepares Annual Operating Plan | | X | | X | |
| Prepares Annual Budget | | | | X | |
| Oversees budget variance and performance reporting | | | | | X |
| **BUSINESS DEVELOPMENT** | | | | | |
| Serves as public relations officer | X | | | | |
| Oversees marketing and advertising | X | | | | |
| Represents company at industry and community functions | X | | | | X |
| Develops business relationships with new clients | X | | | | X |
| Develops additional business with existing clients | X | | | | X |
| Ensures relationships with regulatory agencies | X | | | | X |
| Ensures client satisfaction with the firm's performance. | X | | | | X |
| **ORGANIZATIONAL** | | | | | |
| Establishes company culture and serves spokesperson to employees | | X | | X | |
| Approves Human Resources policies and procedures | | X | | | |
| Designs organizational structure | | X | | X | |
| Ensures executive succession plans for key positions | | | X | | |
| Recruits and hires senior management | | | X | | |
| Develops incentive compensation systems for senior management | | | X | | |
| Develops company-wide salary administration system | | | | | X |
| Oversees company-wide career planning programs | | | | | X |
| Oversees training and development programs | | | | | X |
| Ensures coordination and communications between all offices | | | | | X |
| **OPERATIONAL AND CLIENT SERVICE** | | | | | |
| Oversees all client engagements and project execution | | | | | X |
| Ensures client satisfaction with project services | | | | | X |
| Oversees staffing assignments on client projects | | | | | X |
| Assures quality control measurement systems for client satisfaction | | | | | X |
| Oversees operating standards, procedures and forms management | | | | | X |
| **BOARD OF DIRECTORS AND SHAREHOLDERS** | | | | | |
| Recommends Strategic Plan for Board approval | X | | | | |
| Recommends Annual Operating Plan for Board approval | X | | | | |
| Recommends individuals to Board for election as officers | X | | | | |
| Recommends mergers and acquisitions for Board approval | X | | | | |
| Presents financial results to Board and shareholders | X | | | | |
| Recommends eligibility of new shareholders to Board of Directors | X | | | | |

We then met to compare answers and negotiate any differences of viewpoint. It turned out the two executives' viewpoints were fairly similar. For any differences, we managed to achieve consensus on where accountability would lie.

The sample matrix illustrates how the executives in this case were able to structure their responsibilities to enable most decisions to be made by one person or the other. For some decisions, the input of the other person was requested before making a decision. In only three areas, the executives were required to make a joint decision.

In addition, for certain activities they agreed that both of them had responsibility. For example, they agreed that both had the responsibility to communicate strategic intent statements to their employees frequently.

Each had responsibilities for business development, so in this section both executives needed to be able to act on their own without input from the other.

The executives' intention was to maximize their personal accountability and freedom to act, while identifying the critical decisions that were more appropriate to make together.

As a result of using this tool, each executive was able to stake out his own territory by deciding *who* was responsible for *what*. Each was able to know in advance *when* he was free to act on his own and *when* he had agreed to collaborate, either by merely providing the other party input or by making the decision jointly. For both of these executives, this simple tool helped them work out an arrangement they were pleased with.

The same type of instrument can be used to determine responsibilities of individual executives versus standing committees. Additionally, I often use this tool to help CEOs and boards of directors distinguish the relative responsibilities and accountability for making decisions.

## The People Aspects of Managing Your Brand

Because the word *Who* directly conveys the dimension of people, in this chapter we have discussed the critical importance of leadership in growing your business. Let's take this a step further and apply the question "Who are we?" to the position of your business in the marketplace. Consider the question "Who are we as a brand?"

To demonstrate the concept quickly, I ask my audiences which automobile comes to mind when they think of safety. Typically everyone responds with Volvo. Sometimes I reverse the question and ask what comes to mind when they think of Volvo, and everyone responds with "safety."

Volvo has worked hard to create top-of-mind awareness in both directions—from product name to brand attribute, and also from brand attribute to product name. This certainly has a beneficial impact on brand positioning.

An interesting exercise to ask your team would be to fill in the blanks of this question: "If Volvo equals safety, and safety equals Volvo, then [*your company*] equals [*primary brand attribute*]." If you were to fill in that blank with a key attribute of your company's brand, would the expression work equally well in reverse, such as: "When the market thinks of [your key brand attribute], do they think of [your company]?" That's a far more difficult goal to achieve.

What key brand attribute first comes to mind when your company's name is mentioned? What would the marketplace say? What would your most important customer say? What would your employees say? If the answer to this is not clear to your own team, how can you expect your brand to be clear in your marketplace?

Become very deliberate in deciding which brand position you and your team want to create. If managed deliberately, your company's *brand equity* can become its greatest asset. After the last twenty years of books on branding, this has become a generally accepted principle. The question is, what impact does the leadership of your company have on your brand equity? What impact do your employees have?

Consciously choosing which brand and company image you want to project is a challenge, as is managing your brand. The marketplace as well as your employees pay close attention to whether the behavior of individuals supports the intended branding message. The key is for everyone to "walk the talk" of your intended brand. Otherwise your brand equity may shift from being a positive to a negative factor in building your company's overall value. Regardless of what you say your intention is, the marketplace *always* has the ability to sense the truth.

The quest for clarity around the question *Who* compels us to consider all aspects of how branding messages get communicated. Consider the founders of your business or organization. *Who* are they as people? What were the founding principles they promoted in beginning your business? What is the connection between these individuals and your company brand?

As your business grew, did the nature of these answers change? Are there elements of your identity that shifted as more key persons were added? How does every person in your company contribute to your brand?

### Case History: Goodmans Interior Structures

Goodmans, a client in Phoenix, has a powerful theme that describes its culture: "Everything matters." This extends from how its president typically sends thank-you notes to customers and recognition notes to employees, to how its receptionist always smiles when you walk in the door, to how every employee acts every day. The attention to detail in how people interact is directly building the company's intended strategic position of "the *ultimate* experience in service from any contractor."

Even if you hire the best marketing company in the world, whether or not your leaders and employees directly support an intended brand position through everyday behavior will make the difference in the brand equity you create.

To conclude this chapter, I will restate the opening premise about the question *Who*: it's all about people.

## Key Lessons of This Chapter

1. The question *Who* addresses the subject of people. Quality people make a difference in every business.

2. The leadership in your company is vital to a healthy culture. Great leaders demonstrate great personal, interpersonal, professional, and strategic skills.

3. The image of your company and how key people act contribute to your brand equity. This is your most precious asset.

## Actions to Take

1. Ensure your company has the highest caliber of people, especially at the senior leadership level.

2. Provide a mechanism for executive development and ongoing progression for key employees.

3. Clarify responsibility and accountability for decision-making, so the role people have is clear.

4. Identify how the leaders and employees in your company can directly add value to building your company's brand.

## You Have Completed the Strategic Questions

By now, having completed Section II in this book, you have addressed the four key strategic questions for your business:

1. You have reexamined your niche and alternative **choices** and have gained new insight into *which* business to be in, *which* market to target, *which* products and services to sell, and through *which* distribution channels to sell them.

2. You have examined *why* you are in this business and the **purpose** and motives behind your thinking, and have clarified the key decision criteria you will use in making your most important decisions.

3. You have explored *where* your industry is headed and where your business is headed, and you have created a vision for your future market **position**.

4. You have looked into the soul of your business and you clearly understand *who* you are in your industry in terms of your brand and the key **people** who set the tone, culture, and identity of your business.

## The Operational Questions Are Next

At this point, you are likely to have uncovered some of the key strategic issues facing your business and have begun clarifying your strategic direction. The next three chapters, *What, How,* and *When,* will help you with operational matters and executing your strategic intent.

# SECTION III

---

## THE OPERATIONAL QUESTIONS

*"The #1 reason that stops people from getting what they want is lack of focus. People who focus on **what** they want prosper. Those who don't, struggle."*
—Jack Canfield, Mark Victor Hansen, Les Hewitt
*The Power of Focus*

## Becoming Operationally Efficient

As pointed out in Section II and the framework below, *What, How,* and *When* are the operational efficiency questions.

### THE SEVEN QUESTIONS™ FRAMEWORK
Components of Intention

| | | Question | Element | Conveys |
|---|---|---|---|---|
| Strategic Effectiveness | | 1. Which? | Choice | Niche |
| | | 2. Why? | Purpose | Values |
| | | 3. Where? | Position | Vision |
| | | 4. Who? | People | Culture |
| Operational Efficiency | | 5. What? | Results | Goals |
| | | 6. How? | Process | Method |
| | | 7. When? | Action | Timing |

© Copyright 2009 Strategic Development Corporation

The following chapters point out the importance of the role of management in transforming a strategic plan into an operational plan as a focus for management.

Being operationally efficient begins with clarifying *what* specific results or outcomes are desired. It means having clear goals and objectives that drive your business.

It also requires developing the best process for *how* to accomplish a desired result and identifying the strategies and tactics to be used.

Operational efficiency calls for developing an execution plan that states *when* action will be taken, with clear accountability for all parties. Action plans require an understanding of the proper sequence and timing of activities such that they are executed in the right order to achieve a desired outcome.

Addressing these types of questions helps us focus on what you need to grow your business. When our immediate attention is on doing things right, all aspects of quality begin to improve.

To be able to focus your intention and grow your business, your leadership and management team must be both strategically effective and operationally efficient. By addressing the questions raised in the following three chapters, you will be well on your way to achieving this result.

# CHAPTER 6: WHAT?
## The Element of Results

*Don't tell people **how** to do things; tell them **what** to do and let them surprise you with their results.*

—George S. Patton

## The Essence of What Conveys Results

The question *What* reflects the subject of achievement. When we ask, "*What* are we going to accomplish?" we are on a quest for specificity. A level of specificity is often captured in a goal, objective, target, metric, outcome, or deliverable as a *result*.

Clients using The Seven Questions often inquire about whether the question *"How much?"* serves the purpose of providing specificity. My response is yes, the question does work to provide a metric in setting a goal. For example, when I ask a client, "What do you want to accomplish in profits?" I also could have asked, "How much profit do you want?" Either question would cause the client to think through a level of achievement.

In the English language, there are only seven one-word questions to make up The Seven Questions, so the question *How much?* serves as a "subset" of the question *What*. When teaching this planning framework to European clients, I expand the framework to include eight questions. This is because in certain other languages *How much* is conveyed by one word: *Cuanto* in Spanish, *Quanto* in Italian, *Combien* in French, and *Wieviel* in German. For translation to more languages, refer to the Appendix.

What is therefore important is not the wording of the question itself (i.e., *What* or *How much*), but the *meaning* behind the question: an intended level of achievement. Helping you achieve clarity of your intention is what this book is all about.

> *The manager asks **how** and **when**; the leader asks **what** and **why**."*
> —Warren Bennis

Many years ago this concept was reinforced for me when I met Lou Tice, founder of The Pacific Institute. Lou notes that people are *teleological* by nature. That is to say, we are basically goal-driven.

As humans, we respond well to understanding a specific desired outcome. Once an objective we believe to be valuable is fixed in our mind, suddenly all resources important to achieving that objective begin to materialize.

Have you ever noticed that once you have determined a specific outcome you simply *must* achieve, people begin to mysteriously appear in your life who somehow support your achievement? Over the last thirty years, many of my clients have conveyed countless examples of this phenomenon. Without question, there is substance to the expression, "As a man thinketh."

### Case History: Starbucks

In 1992 at a Starbucks strategy retreat, I asked the team what specific level of achievement they would like to accomplish in the next seven years. Howard Schultz was quick to formulate his goal: "2,000 by 2000," meaning 2,000 retail stores by the year 2000. (At the time there were fewer than 200 stores in existence.) He added a second goal: to achieve $1 billion in revenues by the year 2000.

Orin Smith exclaimed, "Howard, that's a tall order on retail stores and revenues, given our current rate of expansion."

Howard responded, "You are absolutely right. And I believe we now have the executive team to achieve it, and if we commit to doing so we *will* achieve it." Howard was unequivocal in his belief and expression.

By FY(fiscal year)1999, Starbucks had 2,500 retail stores in 13 countries and generated $1.7 billion in revenues, surpassing both goals set in 1992. By FY2000, revenues had grown to $2.2 billion.

## Example of Clarity: President John F. Kennedy

I remember listening to President John F. Kennedy express his clear intention on space travel: "I believe this nation should commit itself to achieving the goal, before this decade is out, of landing a man on the moon and returning him safely to the Earth."

This simply-stated single goal rallied an entire nation to achieve something that, at the time, was viewed to be nearly impossible. People did not know how the goal would be accomplished at the time it was set; all they knew was the result President Kennedy was seeking.

## What Do *You* Want to Achieve?

What do you most want to achieve in your business? How do you measure the success of your business? These are such simple questions, yet most businesses have no clarity about their intentions.

I recently engaged the CEO of a prominent business on this question. His response: "To grow."

"Grow to what level?" I asked.

"I don't want to commit to a specific level," he responded.

"Why not?" I asked.

He told me he didn't really believe in goal setting.

"You have a concern about setting goals," I said.

He told me in confidence that by doing so he would have to make a commitment and be held accountable by his board of directors. He was also fearful that his employees might be disillusioned if the company did not achieve a huge goal. Fear seemed to dominate his concerns.

I asked, "What would happen if some of your best producers were to leave the company?"

He told me that would be disastrous for the firm.

I shared with him that in my experience, often the best employees will leave a firm for reasons unrelated to compensation.

I went on to explain that in exit interviews with employees of another company, excellent employees had conveyed to me that they had lost trust in the relationship with the firm, the CEO lacked vision and commitment, and the firm seemed to just exist without intentions or something it was moving toward.

Just as a bricklayer identifies with a cathedral he is building, not just the bricks he is laying, employees want to have a context in which they see themselves. It is such a context that vision, goals, mission, and values help form. Without strategic intent, a business lacks the very context employees rally around.

*You can't hit a **target** you cannot see, and you cannot see a target you do not have.*
—Zig Ziglar

## Don't Be Afraid to Set Great Goals!

If this chapter finds you, or your company, without any meaningful and challenging goals, try the following exercise. Begin with a blank sheet of paper and write down every subject that comes to mind that you feel might lend itself to a goal.

Next, identify the major stakeholders in your business. Key stakeholders might include customers, alliance partners, investors, suppliers, employees, the local community, and so on.

For each group of stakeholders, identify potential goal subjects. Senior managers might have profit margins as their primary subject of interest. Shareholders might have more interest in return on equity or share price. A goal such as "Receive the award for Best Place to Work" might be valuable to employees. A goal of "Raise customer satisfaction ratings from 95 percent to 98.5 percent" might be important to increase customer loyalty. You get the picture. Which goals are most important to each stakeholder group?

Next, ask yourself how well you know whether the draft goals you have in mind really represent the goals others would desire from each stakeholder. Be sure to do your homework and find out the truth to avoid incorrect assumptions. It is amazing how often we assume we know what others really want, when in fact their thoughts may be quite different.

Once you identify the appropriate goal to achieve, on which both provider and receiver have reached consensus, then determine how to express that goal. Does the goal lend itself to being quantified with some measure? If appropriate, create a metric and track your success against that metric.

For example, if your intention is to manage risks by diversifying your customer base, an appropriate goal might be: "Generate business opportunities with new market segments such that our main customer, XYZ, represents less than ___ percent of total revenues by December 31, [year]."

Generally, people respond better to goals that have a time frame. Once again, use your judgment about the specificity desired by each stakeholder group, just as long as the goal is clear and compelling.

If you have spent the time to set a goal, be sure to track your success and report progress to interested parties. Remember, the purpose of the exercise in goal setting is to provide a context for those who have an interest in knowing your intentions. You are highly likely to find that your draft goals will need to be modified over time, either in subject, format, or magnitude. This is normal. Avoid frustration. You are learning! Just keep getting better and better at the practice of clarifying your intentions.

I have often heard the concern: "*Why* bother setting goals if the world keeps changing? We'll only be disappointed." In my experience, the probability of achievement is far greater when goals are set than when there are no goals.

## *How* to Write Effective Goals and Objectives

The purpose of establishing goals (long-term) and objectives (short-term) is to plan the achievement of something specific that is worthwhile. Goals are most effective when they are specific and to the point. Used effectively, goals:

- Result in improved communication about the outcomes to be accomplished.
- Provide a measurement device to help evaluate performance and provide incentive compensation or base-pay increases.
- Increase the probability of superior performance by focusing thoughts on the desired outcome.

It is important that goals be challenging and realistic. Objectives that are too easy to achieve do not serve their purpose in creating a challenge. On the other hand, objectives that are unrealistic and are never attained can serve to de-motivate an individual and produce the opposite effect of what was intended.

The following list has resulted from many years of working with CEOs on establishing goals for their businesses. By adhering to these "top ten" criteria, you will increase the probability that goals will be taken seriously and achieved.

## GOAL SETTING
### Criteria for Establishing Effective Goals

1. Is the subject matter *meaningful* to achieve?

2. Does it have a *single* theme?

3. Is it *compatible* with the visions, missions and values?

4. Is the objective stated in *results*-oriented language?

5. Is the objective *challenging* and achievable?

6. Does the objective have a *metric* to gauge success?

7. Is there a *time frame* associated with the objective?

8. Is it clear, *concise*, and understandable?

9. Does it provide *what* only (and not *how* and *why*)?

10. Can performance be *evaluated* by an outside party?

> *Goals are not only absolutely necessary to motivate us. They are essential to really keep us alive.*
> —Robert H. Schuller

## Sampling of Client Goals

The following are examples of goals that clients of mine have set for different subjects.

- Revenue: To generate $10M in sales of our new product within three years of launch date.
- Growth: To grow $20B in assets within three years.
- Portfolio: To diversify such that no one customer represents more than 25 percent of our total revenue.
- Margins: To maintain current margins during the next five years by absorbing supplier price increases while initiating cost reductions.
- Market Share: To achieve a minimum of 12 percent market share in each major metropolitan region.
- Geographic Expansion: To open an office in the San Francisco Bay Area by the end of this year.
- Organizational: To hire a CEO within 90 days of closing on funding.
- Facilities: To complete all renovations before the annual shareholders meeting.
- Product: To receive our second order for a personalized executive submarine.
- Succession: To have identified two candidates for each of the C-level positions before the Board Strategy Retreat held in Q4.
- Merger: To sign the Definitive Agreement just prior to the industry convention next year.
- Cost Reduction: To reduce manufacturing costs by 7 percent within three years.

- Cost Avoidance: To negotiate 90-day extension of cost increases with major suppliers.
- Retail: Increase same-store sales growth at the fastest rate in the industry for the next ten years.

The goal you want to achieve might reflect an outcome that doesn't lend itself to numbers. You may have a special state of being, either physically or spiritually, that you want to achieve. What is the single most important objective you want your business to achieve? How visible is this goal—or image of what it will be like when the goal has been achieved—to all of those responsible for achieving the goal?

## Storyboarding

The visuals you use to describe your strategies can take any form, including sketches and charts. These visuals can be helpful if they quickly summarize your intention. The combination of words and pictures to illustrate this technique is called a storyboard, developed at Walt Disney Studios.

Years ago I created a sketch on a yellow pad to envision a future "Business Platform" based on The Seven Questions. This helped me share my story with clients and friends to get their feedback. That original yellow page has since been upgraded with better graphics shown on the next page. It continues to help me convey my vision on a single piece of paper.

Is there a story you want to tell about the vision you hold for your own business? How would you sketch that vision in a collage to tell your story quickly? Does your sketch tell a story of how the value of your business will increase over time?

In addition to selling more products or services to generate more earnings, what other factors are in your storyboard for growing the value of your business?

# SAMPLE STORYBOARD

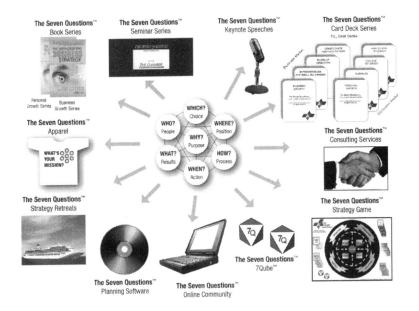

© Copyright 2009 Strategic Development Corporation

## Build Your Strategic Equity

Many of my clients are privately held corporations that seek to increase the value of their firm. Through discussions about valuations with my associates over many years, we developed a model to describe the components of value, which we refer to as *strategic equity.*

In addition to the financial equity you see on your balance sheet as net worth, four other factors contribute to strategic equity from the viewpoint of a buyer:

- Brand equity
- Systems equity
- Human equity
- Alliance equity

## STRATEGIC EQUITY
### Strengthen Each Component of Equity in Order to Increase Overall Company Value

© Copyright 2009 Strategic Development Corporation

The converse is also true; if your business is weak in its brand, systems, human, or alliance equity, this will translate to a lower value for these elements and overall strategic equity. If your strategic equity components are not strong, when it comes time for funding the business for growth, the cost of capital may be higher. Let's look at each of these components of value in more detail.

- **Brand equity** represents the incremental value to your business resulting from your brand and company image that would not exist without your brand. This may include the effects of marketing, customer service, consumer loyalty, and a whole range of other factors. A business that has a more powerful brand increases its strategic equity, which translates to increasing the probability of future cash flows and a higher company value.

- **Systems equity** encompasses how strong your infrastructure is in how you do business. For example, IT (information technology) systems, MRP (materials requirements planning), CRM (customer relationship management), operational procedures, equipment, and other "machinery" that help your business run are all important in strengthening the systems equity component of value.

- **Human equity** addresses the leadership talent, technical know-how, professional expertise, and other skills and experiences that are represented by your team. The better the caliber of talent your business has, the more confidence customers and investors have in creating future cash flows, therefore the higher your human equity. If you agree with the concept "your people are your best assets," what attention do you give to developing talent in critical areas of your business?

- **Alliance equity** is an extension of human equity and represents the talent of other companies with which you have strategic alliances. Starbucks' joint ventures with companies like Costco and Pepsi, which also enjoy excellent strategic equity, are such examples. All three businesses are strong, so their alliances build the strategic equity of each company.

Set goals and develop strategies to increase the strength of each element of strategic equity, thereby increasing the overall value of your business.

## Rewarding Yourself for Achievement

As you set goals, plan to reward yourself for achievement. And keep reminding yourself of the goal with a photo, sketch, or some other visual of the reward. Remember, a picture is worth a thousand words.

A client of mine, a small-business owner in Texas, set a five-year earnings goal for himself. Throughout the five years, he kept a photo on his wall of a gorgeous red BMW M3 he had always wanted. He called me recently to express his delight in achieving his goal and getting his reward.

This example of purchasing an expensive vehicle may sound extraordinary, but it is all relative to the situation. For most people, a far smaller reward may be quite sufficient. The point remains the same: If you or your employees work hard to achieve a desired outcome, reward yourself and others for your accomplishment. It will create a desire to achieve the next major goal.

## Celebrate Achievement of Team Goals

What do you do when you achieve an important goal for yourself? As you have read earlier in this chapter, some people treat themselves to something special. What any one of us considers special for a given achievement might range from something simple like a dinner out with our spouse to something more elaborate like a vacation in Hawaii.

For your business, ask your team what might be an appropriate way to celebrate outstanding success. In my client photo album, I have photos of La Marzocco of Florence, Italy, celebrating the executive team's success with a ski trip in Switzerland. WeatherShield Coatings of Orlando, Florida, celebrated its success with a river rafting trip in Georgia. Sunbelt Distribution in Houston, Texas, celebrated success with its dealers by taking them salmon fishing in Kenai, Alaska.

Other client celebrations of team achievements have included scuba diving, salmon fishing, fly fishing and snowmobiling, waterskiing, horseback riding, and boating and cruising.

Today's economic environment calls for being prudent with every dollar. Exotic vacations are being replaced with local getaways. If the amount of money budgeted for company or departmental celebrations gets reduced by a financial scalpel, simply choose less expensive venues with fun activities that boost company morale. You don't have to spend a lot of money to celebrate your team's achievements.

How will you and your team celebrate your next major success? What special memories could you create with the team that made the success possible? What photos or videos could you arrange to create memories that build your culture for achieving great things?

If you have a major company goal you want your team to achieve, ask each team member what an appropriate means of celebration might be if the goal is achieved. Whatever the answer, make sure you and your team celebrate whenever some great goal is achieved. This will boost the probability of recurring success.

## Key Lessons of This Chapter

1. The question *What* is rooted in achievement—creating a desirable specific result. It is a dimension of thought that differentiates humans from other species. To be able to contemplate *what* you want to achieve in business, or for that matter *what* you want to achieve in your life, is a source of energy that helps us feel alive.

2. It is said that anything you contemplate with clarity and greatness of purpose is possible to achieve. Crystallizing your thoughts about *what* you want to accomplish is the

first important step toward achievement. For others to respond with resources to help you achieve your goal, the goal also must be in harmony with delivering something good to society. If you believe the goal you are achieving will have a favorable impact on the world and bring good to those involved, you will simply be amazed at how fast you get results.

3. When you achieve major goals in your life, celebrate!

*You are successful the moment you start moving toward a worthwhile goal.*
—Chuck Carlson

## Action Items

1. I dare you to jump into your own business and express goals of the highest magnitude! Set goals for your business, your career, and other goals you may have for your business contribution to the community or society as a whole.

2. Find others who share your passion about your business.

3. Ask yourself these questions:
   - *What* great achievement do I aspire to for my business?
   - *What* do I want my business to have contributed to the world?
   - *What* do I want my business to be known for?

## You've Mastered Five Questions—Two More to Go!

You are almost there. Before moving on, take stock of what you have already accomplished:

1.  You have reexamined your niche and alternative **choices** and have gained new insight into *which* business to be in, *which* market to target, *which* products and services to sell, and through *which* distribution channels to sell them.

2.  You have examined *why* you are in this business and the **purpose** and motives behind your thinking, and have clarified the key decision criteria you use in making your most important decisions.

3.  You have explored *where* your industry is headed, a **vision** for your business, and where you want to position your business in the marketplace.

4.  You have looked into the soul of your business and you clearly understand *who* you are in your industry in terms of your brand and the key **people** who set the tone, culture, and identity of your business.

5.  You have come to conclusions on *what* **results** you want to accomplish, have identified critical areas for achievement, and have set major long-term goals and annual objectives.

By now you must be eager to learn how to put into motion all you want to pursue. In Chapter 7—*How?* You will be given the opportunity to do just that. Read on!

# CHAPTER 7: HOW?
## The Element of Process

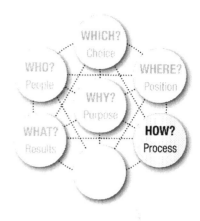

*Leaders on the front lines of any industry must strive for simplicity and clarity if they hope to inspire and motivate employees, customers, or shareholders.*

—Carmine Gallo
*Ten Simple Secrets of the World
Greatest Business Communicators*

## The Essence of *How* Conveys Process

The question *How* conveys a process, method, approach, or strategy for accomplishing a result. When we consider how to do something, we engage our cerebral cortex by contemplating alternative methods to guide our actions.

We can apply the element of *how* at a macro, high-altitude, strategic effectiveness level, or at a micro, on-the-ground, operational efficiency level. Let's take the strategic level first.

## Strategic Initiatives

A strategic initiative is a high-level action taken over a period of time to better position your business. While this phrase is often used in large corporations, the concept can apply to a small business as well.

What follows is a story of building the value of a family-held business over a fifty-year period by a series of strategic decisions.

## Case History: A Family-Owned Business

Two brothers owned a very small store selling aluminum windows. The following strategic decisions changed the course of this business.

- Mylar window shades were added to the product line for customers who wanted to reduce heat, glare, or fading of fabrics resulting from the intensity of sunlight coming through their windows.
- For customers that did not want to use shades, a DuPont franchise was purchased to enable window tinting to be installed directly on a window with a liquid polymer coating that dried to a thin film.
- The business expanded its market from residential windows to commercial and industrial windows.
- A 3M franchise was acquired to provide tinting using aluminized plastic sheeting that could adhere to the window and provide greater reflectivity.
- The business expanded beyond commercial and residential markets into the auto tint business.
- Additional suppliers of tinting materials were engaged to satisfy the demand from all market segments.
- The business trained other entrepreneurs how to be successful in creating their own dealerships which lead to enlarging the business model to include distribution.

Today this business is a large distributor of tinting products and services for the dealer network it created.

The best way to identify potential strategic initiatives that may help your company grow is to first identify issues critical to the long-term viability of your business. Remember, a critical issue can be either a threat or an opportunity that can have a substantial impact on your business. For each major critical issue, determine what type of initiative could help you and your team to better manage, or resolve, the issue.

One word of caution about strategic initiatives: Try to select your most important initiatives. Generally there are only a few critical issues that can make, or break, a company. You cannot tackle everything and make substantial progress. Select wisely.

In order to ensure you are considering the broadest source of potential avenues to choose from, a little brainstorming might help. Try the following experiment.

Think of any subject of interest for which you would like to achieve a certain outcome. Then generate a list of as many different methods as possible to achieve that outcome.

Suppose, for example, you want to manufacture a new product. What might come to mind are the various methods or manufacturing processes. Now set aside the question of *how* to make the product, and identify what function your product actually performs.

This exercise is helpful to expand our breadth of thinking when it comes to developing strategies. Because we are all creatures of habit, we tend to repeat patterns of familiar *how-to* thoughts. Brainstorming helps awaken the mind.

If you first define *what* value your customer wants your product or service to deliver, you are in a better position to develop the strategies of *how* to achieve that result.

## Value Engineering

The same process of identifying value can be applied to any subject. As a young engineer at Rutgers University, I was taught a process called *value engineering.* In an attempt to discover other answers to the question *How*, we were asked to identify the basic value of an object in question. After doing so, we were challenged to go beyond the obvious and contemplate other devices that might deliver the same value.

Let's suppose your company makes glass tumblers. If you define your product—your business—as tableware, you might want to extend your offering to include dishes and silverware. If, however, you define your business as products that hold liquids, you might consider tumblers or larger plastic containers made out of materials other than glass. If you define your business as products made from glass, your product line could encompass a very broad range of items.

Applying this line of thinking to your business, what value does the product or service you currently offer deliver? Your conclusion will lead you to grow your business potential by offering products or services that are complementary to the functional value you are currently delivering. Seeking answers to the question *How* is a matter of letting go of assumptions, resistance, and constrained thinking.

You have probably seen the exercise that follows but if you have forgotten the answer, you will have fun trying to refresh your memory. Here's a hint: This clearly illustrates thinking outside the box! Connect all nine dots by drawing only four straight lines, without lifting your pen from the paper. *(The answer is in the Appendix.)*

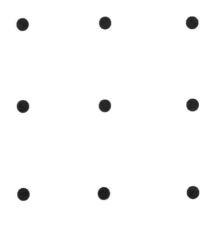

## Business Development Processes

Given the goals and objectives you've established in the preceding chapter, what processes or methods could you engage to achieve your goal?

For *your* business, what picture would you draw to illustrate *how* business is developed in your company? What is the relationship between the sales of each of your products? Does one lead to another, or are they each independent of one another?

## SAMPLE BUSINESS DEVELOPMENT
### Process for Building Alliances

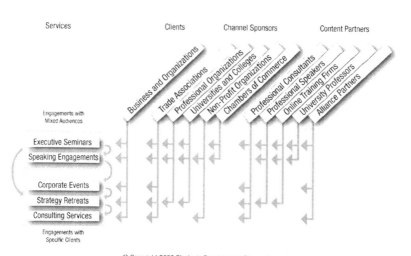

© Copyright 2009 Strategic Development Corporation

What broad network do you rely on to generate referrals to your business, other than your existing or former customers or clients? See if you can map out the processes to tell a picture of *how* business flows.

As an example, at Strategic Development Corporation we provide various *services*, including executive seminars, speaking engagements, corporate events, strategy retreats, and consulting services. While most of our business is referred to us by satisfied *clients*, we also receive referrals from a network of professional resources.

In the sample storyboard on business development, some groups serve as *channel sponsors*—groups that are in a position to "channel" their constituents to my firm. Examples of these groups are trade associations, professional organizations, universities, nonprofit organizations, and chambers of commerce. My active involvement with these organizations sometimes leads to referrals for services.

My firm also partners with other subject-matter experts to co-develop content for specific audiences. These *content partners* may be other professional consultants, speakers, trainers, professors, or other alliance partners.

Having a map of *how* to develop your business and an understanding of whom to network with can help you make your time as productive as possible. Networking alone does not work if you are not networking with the right audience.

Once you have identified the important relationships that help your business flourish, consider how you can deliver value to each of these relationships.

Business development is always a two-way street. The more value you provide to your most valued resources, the greater the value that will be returned to you. Although this doesn't always hold true with every relationship, I find that in general, what goes around does, in fact, come back around.

### Case History: Cranium

The entrepreneurs who created the popular board game Cranium first experienced tremendous disappointment and frustration in marketing their game because they were trying to do so through traditional channels such as Toys"R"Us, Target, Wal-Mart, and other major retailers that sell board games.

The creators began to challenge their assumption that games needed to be sold through traditional game retailers.

Their epiphany came one day as they sat in a Starbucks store and realized that Starbucks' customers were the type of people who might appreciate their game. The creators collaborated with Starbucks to market the game through the coffeehouses. This strategy of relaxing their assumptions on *how* they would market their product enabled Cranium to achieve a level of sales that otherwise would have been impossible.

## High-Altitude Strategies and Ground-Level Tactics

The question *How* can be addressed at both the micro and macro level. At ground level, the *How* question is often expressed as tactics—specific actions. It is also in your best interest to address the *How* at the "40,000 foot" strategic level. You might be surprised at what you can see.

Address the question of whether your business should grow through traditional means by itself, or whether to consider joint ventures with other companies with similar interests with which you form a strategic alliance agreement, or whether to pursue a merger or acquisition. Begin by thinking in the broadest terms possible and envision five, ten, or even twenty years ahead.

Once you have a long-term picture in your mind, come back to ground level and link the present with the future. What specific, tactical plan will you launch during the next ninety days that will begin bringing you closer to your long-term vision? *How* will these actions be coordinated, *who* will be held accountable for results, and *how* will your progress be monitored?

## Strategic Alignment

Once your strategic intent statements have been crafted, your next step is to align all facets of your business with your mission, values, vision, and goals.

First ensure that your business and sales function is directly aligned with the marketplace and the needs of your customers. This means your product or service must provide the solution needed to resolve a customer's need or want.

## STRATEGIC ALIGNMENT
### Align All Functions to the Needs of the Marketplace and to Your Strategic Intention

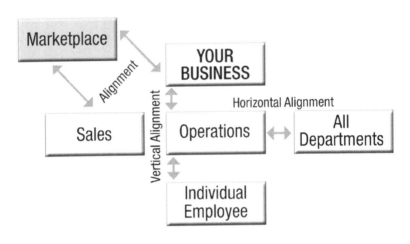

© Copyright 2009 Strategic Development Corporation

Vertically, ensure that the mission and goals of every department and employee are aligned with the mission and goals of your company.

Horizontally, ensure that all departments and divisions are appropriately aligned. This requires that all division or department managers understand how their respective functions are linked with all other departments or divisions.

When the process of strategic alignment is working well, everyone throughout your company should understand how their respective functions fit with the bigger picture.

This means that the purpose of every group is aligned to serve the broader purpose of the company in serving its customers. It also means that all areas are aligned to achieve goals important to the company and your customer base.

## Organizational Alignment

It is in your best interests to align all facets of managing people with the strategic intent of your business.

This begins with determining *which* organizational structure—the reporting relationships and accountability for managing people—will be needed to carry out the strategies you have developed.

Many executives make the mistake of keeping the organizational structure design constant, even though there may be major changes brewing in their company or in their industry. Continually challenge yourself to organize all of your resources in a manner that best meets the objectives you have established.

Monitor when there are changes in the needs of the marketplace, shifts in the demographics of your customers, evolution of company culture, changes in where people work, and so on.

Based on the changes you are observing, continually ask whether the way you are organized best suits achievement of customer satisfaction goals or other company objectives. Adjust your structure as necessary to accommodate the resources needed for focusing on the right issues.

Once the organizational structure has been determined, seek to clarify *who* is responsible for *what* and *how* decisions will be made (for example, refer to the Authority Matrix in

Chapter 5). Ensure that the *how* of decision making is clear, with agreements on the level of authority for each layer of management.

Similarly, company, departmental, and individual goals and objectives should all be aligned.

## ORGANIZATIONAL ALIGNMENT
### Align All Aspects of Managing People
### to Your Strategic Intention

© Copyright 2009 Strategic Development Corporation

*How* you conduct performance reviews and nurture career planning and development should also be aligned with your business strategy.

Periodically conduct an organizational alignment "audit" to determine if any aspects of managing people are misaligned.

This will help you spot areas that are either not working well together or are working against fulfillment of your strategic intention.

## Organizational Design

How is *your* business currently organized? Which dimensions of organization have you chosen? For example, some companies organize based on:

- traditional functions (e.g., manufacturing, sales, operations, finance, human resources)
- geographic responsibility (e.g., cities or regions)
- product, program, or project responsibility
- vertical markets and segments (e.g., energy, commercial banking, long-term acute-care hospitals)
- customer segmentation (e.g., private banking for wealthy individuals)
- client situation (e.g., early-stage technology companies)
- existing versus new business (e.g., an executive who is responsible for exploring only that which does *not* exist as a current product or service, while other executives carry out the business that does currently exist)

Ask yourself the following questions:

- Is the basis of *how* we are currently organized furthering our ability to manage critical issues?
- *How* has responsibility for managing critical issues been assigned with clear accountability?
- *How* will the current structure evolve over time to address issues that are emerging?

### Case Histories on Alignment

The following case histories represent real client examples where various facets of a business were out of alignment and executives took action to correct the problem.

- A bank was focused heavily on asset growth with less scrutiny on asset quality. Loan officers were heavily compensated for aggressive sales practices with less attention to conservative underwriting standards. This inevitably resulted in the bank's demise and being taken over by a larger bank.

- A manufacturer of Italian espresso machines had a sister company for distributing products in the United States. The manufacturer also distributed its products through other means, and the U.S. distributor also represented other manufacturers. There was an overlap of investors, and a president resided over both companies. Owners and executives decided to fully separate the companies so that each business could maximize its growth. The distributor business was eventually sold.

- A furniture distributor reduced its workforce to respond to a decline in revenues. To maintain morale and a strong commitment to customer service, the president developed new mission and company goals, then requested each department head to do the same. In a series of meetings, each department aligned its respective mission and goals to that of the company, and also ensured the job descriptions of employees reflected their commitment to service. In addition, incentive compensation and brand messages were aligned to the new strategic intent statements.

- The managers within a start-up software company were observing how the value of the company's stock was steadily increasing. Although they were paid fair wages and also had traditional stock options with vesting based on employment longevity, the Board C7ompensation Committee awarded nonqualified stock options to managers whereby vesting would be achieved by how fast key company objectives were accomplished. Most managers attained their objectives and as a result vesting of these options accrued faster.

Are there any areas in your business that are out of alignment? If there are none, you are either lucky or very smart. Almost every business I know has some function or program that is no longer aligned to the mission, vision and goals of the company. If this is your situation, take steps to align your business to your strategic intent.

## The Importance of Process and Content

In the business world, if the CEO comes up with the right mission, vision, values, or goals, and does not gain consensus with those expected to carry out these statements, the impact made will not be as high. For this reason, inclusion of others is essential in creating an impact.

Conversely, if the entire organization is involved in a participative manner to create a mission statement that misses the mark, it doesn't matter how many people participated and felt good about their interactions. The right answers (content) are still needed.

Both content and process need to be of the highest value. For this reason, make sure the right issues are tackled and give participants sufficient time to gather relevant information about the issue. If you decide to conduct a business strategy retreat, give consideration to *how* your retreat is designed and facilitated in order to yield the greatest impact.

For example, I just conducted a two-day executive retreat for a large company to determine *how* to restructure its sales functions. While structure was the main focus of the retreat, it was important to begin with a discussion of *what* the company and its sales team wanted to achieve. If these goals were not clear and aligned, any redesigned organizational structure might not have achieved its intended purpose.

## The CPI Formula for Creating Impact

Each of us has only two broad factors to work with to create an impact: (1) the content, and (2) the process by which it is delivered to an audience. This is shown in the CPI formula as follows:

### THE CPI FORMULA
### Improve Impact by Strengthening Delivery

© Copyright 2009 Strategic Development Corporation

The *process* consists of *how* a message is delivered. This includes any factor other than subject matter, such as the speaker's tone of voice, gestures, eye contact, the room setting, and lighting.

Skill in delivering a message can substantially influence the impact on the audience, either favorably or unfavorably. Excellent delivery skills boost impact; poor delivery skills destroy impact. Create the best content you can, then connect with your audience. The effect of process skills on impact can be illustrated in the chart for various levels of content quality.

Extraordinary skills in delivering a message can greatly improve an individual's impact. The election of President Barack Obama was credited, in part, to his ability to inspire his audiences. His use of the Internet as a delivery platform for reaching young adults became a communications model for politicians to emulate. Even though many of President Obama's decisions are controversial, Americans remain impressed with him because of his communication style.

Conversely, poor delivery skills can prevent high-quality content from being received well. On occasion, I will observe a CEO delivering outstanding content to an audience, but failing to achieve the impact desired because of insufficient attention to process considerations.

For example, do you sometimes feel that PowerPoint slides sometimes interfere with a speaker's presentation? I don't just mean poor-quality slides. The slide may have too much

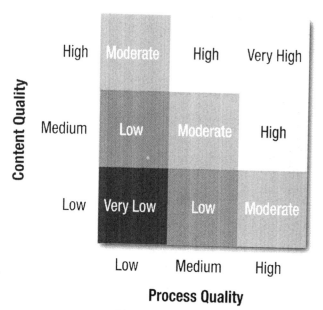

**EFFECT OF PROCESS SKILLS ON IMPACT**
Improve Process Skills of *How* Content Is
Delivered in Order to Increase Impact

© Copyright 2009 Strategic Development Corporation

animation or color effects that cause the audience to focus on the slides instead of the speaker. As a result, the speaker builds less rapport with the audience and thus makes far less impact than expected.

The next time you are presenting your thoughts to a group, become more aware of every process consideration, from the room setting to eye contact to the cheerfulness in your voice. Remember that how you conduct yourself speaks louder than what you say.

## Let Your Subconscious Go to Work

Each of us has had the experience of exerting nonstop effort in trying to figure out how to do something, only to get so frustrated that we've abandoned our goals. Let go! That is to say, let go of racking your brain, but do not abandon your goal. Let your subconscious mind have a turn.

You have probably also had the experience of going to sleep trying to figure out something that has no apparent answer, then awakening with the answer.

Or maybe you've simply stopped trying to figure out the *How* and then you've come upon some extraordinary scene in nature and the answer seems to just "show up" right in front of you.

Your subconscious mind is already well-versed in linking the elements of intention that are derived from The Seven Questions. The elements of results and process, for example, interact by answering the *what* and the *how* in your intention. When your mind is relaxed, it intuitively generates answers to those questions about which you are stumped from trying too hard to resolve.

Your intention goes far beyond your written answers to The Seven Questions; it is a force that is fueled by your clarity and strength of conviction.

We harness this force by having a strong *purpose* and being clear on what we want to *achieve*. If we feel worthy of achieving our goal and it is of value to others, the power of our intention leads us to answers for all other questions.

## Key Lessons of This Chapter

1. The question *how* prompts us to contemplate the process or method by which we will achieve a result. We understand there are many ways to achieve a given outcome, although there may be positive or negative consequences of each alternative method.

2. Business performance can be enhanced by aligning all functions to the strategic intent (mission, values, vision, goals) of the business.

3. All aspects of managing people need to be aligned as well, ranging from organizational design to incentive compensation design.

4. The CPI formula (Content +/- Process = Impact) reminds us that *how* we conduct ourselves has a great impact on the results we achieve.

When Thomas Edison was asked if he felt like a failure after trying for years to invent the light bulb, he responded that he was *successful* in discovering one thousand ways that would not work. His attitude toward his quest for the *How* was most revealing and inspirational.

The next time you experience frustration in figuring out the *How* in your business or life, try something different. See if you can become clearer in answering *Which, Why, Where, Who,* and *What.* And then go about your life. I'll bet the answer to *How* comes to you with lightning speed.

## Actions to Take

1. Before taking action on anything, first be clear of the goal you intend to achieve.

2. Select strategies that are congruent with your decision criteria.

3. Identify three changes you can make to your presentation skills that will increase your impact with your audience.

## You've Almost Completed The Seven Questions

You have almost finished your exercise in both strategic and operational thinking. Before moving on, take stock of what you have already accomplished:

1. You have reexamined your niche and alternative **choices** and have gained new insight into *which* business to be in, *which* market to target, *which* products and services to sell, and through *which* distribution channels to sell them.

2. You have examined *why* you are in this business and the **purpose** and motives behind your thinking, and have clarified the key decision criteria you use in making your most important decisions.

3. You have explored *where* your industry is headed, where your business is headed, and where you want your future market **position** and vision to be.

4. You have looked into the soul of your business and you clearly understand *who* you are in terms of your brand and the key **people** who set the tone, culture, and identity of your business.

5. You have come to conclusions about what **results** you want to accomplish, have identified critical areas for achievement, and have set major long-term goals and annual objectives.

6. You have explored the **process** of *how* you will achieve your goals and have identified key strategies that will help you to be successful.

By now you should be eager to set in motion all of the insights you have gained.

In the final chapter—*When?*—you will build your personal game plan for moving forward. Go for it!

# CHAPTER 8: WHEN?
## The Element of Action

*Bite off more than you can chew,*
*then chew it."*
                                    —Ella Williams

## The Essence of *When* Reflects Action

The question *When* uniquely reflects action, and action reflects time. As humans, we contemplate our lives by reliving the memories of our past and imagining in vivid detail our hopes for the future . . . while too often missing the moment of *now*.

Wake up! How strongly can you focus on this very moment? Become acutely aware of your surroundings. Who is around you? What sounds do you hear? How does it feel physically to be sitting, standing, lying down, running on the treadmill, or whatever else you are doing at the moment as you read this book?

What taste is in your mouth? What scent do you smell? Are you vividly aware that you are alive? How close to the real *now* can you let your mind take you? Can you capture the moment of *now?*

Awareness of your environment is vital to the *When* in your planning. Begin by imagining yourself as your own customer. What experience do your customers have during the first sixty seconds of meeting you? How does this first impression affect their entire experience of your company? Next, remember what it was like for you as an employee during the first sixty minutes after you joined the company. For either experience, are your memories still vivid?

Our first intuitive moments of experience serve to guide us in how we will feel about others in the future. To apply the dimension of time in addressing all the other core questions— *Which, Why, Where, Who, What* and *How*—begin by seeking to understand the critical importance of *time* in your life.

## Action Reflects Time: By *When?*

Consider crafting a dynamic plan for growing your business, instead of a static plan, by merging *When* with the other six core questions.

First, consider addressing the important question, *Which* business are you in? Yes, you've already guessed where I'm going with this. It is one thing to address the answer for the present moment, but another to contemplate additional questions that apply *Which* and *When*. This implies broadening your questions to include a *time frame*, such as:

- *Which* business will you be in one year from now, three years, five years?
- *Which* products and services will you begin to offer, or no longer offer, by a certain *time*?
- *Which* markets will you target over a future period of *time*?
- *Which* types of customers will you pursue during this *time frame*?

Continue this process for each of the remaining core questions. One question might be, How will the *Why* (decision criteria) change over *time*? I can provide an example from my own company.

During the first twenty years of my strategy practice, I rarely accepted out-of-state consulting engagements. Even though I received requests occasionally, I consciously decided to focus on the local market. This enabled me to remain home so I could spend time raising my two boys. Whether it was soccer, wrestling, Boy Scouts, lacrosse, or skiing, the time with my family was worth more than income from out-of-state work.

Whenever I made exceptions, such as for ski resorts in Utah or for Alaska Native corporations, I was able to have my family join me. We had great times salmon fishing and skiing.

Now that my sons are in graduate school and college, I am writing this chapter while en route to a client in Italy. My decision criteria have changed to meet my current circumstances, and now I am free to explore the world.

Whatever your personal or business situation, how should the criteria for business change over time? Are you currently doing things for reasons that should have been changed a long time ago?

Continue this exercise of thought by applying *time* to each key aspect of your business. For example: Where is your industry headed over the next *five years?*

- *When* do you anticipate major forces at play to result in significant events?
- *How long* will it take for a potential competitor to do what you do?
- *How long* will it take for others to catch up and begin offering truly competitive alternatives to what you offer?
- *When* will your industry's ways of conduct change because of technological advances?
- Where is the environment for your industry changing over *time?*
- How is the nature of your marketplace *changing* in relation to types of competitors?

- Are you continually facing the same competitors, or are new types of businesses *emerging* that you never imagined you might compete against?
- How are your competitors' strategies *changing*?
- Who are you in the marketplace now and how do you want this to change in the *future?*
- How will your brand position and image change over *time*?
- How is your customer base *changing* in its composition?
- How has your workforce changed over *time?*

All questions you pose in relation to your strategic intent must be contemplated in relation to the dimension of *time.* By superimposing the question *When* over all other questions, you will gain insight for strategically planning your business and your career.

## Sequencing Activities in Time

It is often the case that the sequence and *timing* of activities are crucial factors in determining which activities to undertake when. Try creating a simple flow chart, like the one that follows, to highlight the major activities you are about to undertake, with a special note of what leads to what.

The following sample illustration could be the flow chart of an entrepreneur who is mapping out what it takes to be ready to apply for a bank loan for operational funding.

Submitting a business plan is a standard requirement, and such a plan would have to be preceded by financial projections. Even before that, market research would be necessary to validate the draft economic model.

## SAMPLE FLOW CHARTS
### Identify the Sequence of Activities

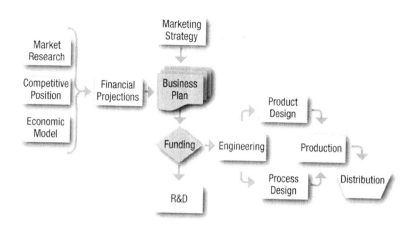

For each activity in your business, note whether activities must occur before or after other activities. Conducting this simple exercise might reveal relationship requirements that you might have overlooked before.

## Critical Path Charts Set Specific Start/Stop Dates

For more complex projects, it may be important to determine the duration of each activity and to map out the sequential relationships, so you are able to determine the overall duration of your project.

By constructing a *critical path,* you will be able to know the early start, late start, early finish, and late finish dates for each activity. This enables you to calculate the overall fastest path to completion that adheres to the required sequence of activities.

A chart completed in this manner may reveal that certain activities lie on the critical path, and therefore the on-time completion of the entire initiative depends on these critical path activities. There may also be more than one critical path.

Other activities may lie outside the critical path and therefore can take advantage of slack time. Slack time is the difference between the early finish and late finish times, which are the earliest a project can finish if everything is done on time and the latest a project can finish to not hold up a completion date.

There are many examples of critical path charts on the Internet. And some consulting firms specialize in planning complex projects that warrant more sophisticated sequencing and process controls.

The value of using a flow chart, critical path chart, or some other means to determine the sequence of activities is that *timing* may greatly affect the overall strategy. The decision whether to pursue a major activity often depends on timing.

Whatever your plans to move your business forward, take the time necessary to understand the timing of major activities in relation to all other forces at play. Sometimes the best strategies need to be sequenced in a certain order to be most effective. An example of the importance of timing is deciding *when* to sell your business.

## Execution Is Everything

Planning by itself has little to no value. Although countless books have been written about planning, it is unfortunate that a perception remains that once a plan is completed, the results will follow. Nonsense! Plans have value only if there is corresponding **action** in the present moment. The future does not exist in reality; it is a notion we have come to accept. *Time,* as well as all *action,* exists only in the present moment.

I am not at all suggesting that planning has no value; on the contrary. I am, however, underscoring that planning without a strong focus on *execution* bears little fruit.

## *When* Reflects Action: Begin the Planning Process

At this point you are probably looking forward to applying what you have learned in this book. The fastest way to begin is to use the Critical Issues Management process discussed in Chapter 2. Here is the chart again.

### CRITICAL ISSUES MANAGEMENT
Manage Issues by Aligning Decisions with Intention

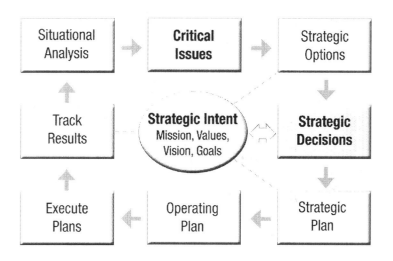

All you have to do to begin taking action is to list all the issues that affect your business. From there, decide which are the most *critical issues*. Evaluate all of your *strategic options*, make *strategic decisions* in content of your *strategic intent*, and from there let your intention and decision drive your *strategic and operating plans*. Simple, right?

Well, it's like learning to do anything. The more you engage in Critical Issues Management and exercise your strategic thinking skills, the easier it becomes. The next thing you know, you're getting better at strategically managing critical threats and opportunities without even realizing it.

When I first began working on strategic planning in the 1970s, most businesses conducted long-term planning every three to five years. In the '80s and '90s many businesses increased the frequency to an annual exercise. These days strategic thinking occurs as often as major external forces greatly affect business—almost daily!

So don't be shy about helping yourself to some good strategic thinking now and then. Find the time each week to reflect on your answers to The Seven Questions and you will find new business opportunities begin to appear everywhere you turn.

### Case History: Goodmans Interior Structures

Goodmans Interior Structures is a successful Herman Miller office furniture dealership with branches in Phoenix and Tucson, Arizona, and Albuquerque, New Mexico. They are taking a phased approach to planning over a five-month period, engaging various groups at each phase, as follows:

- *All employees* – Identify the issues critical in each branch office.
- *Senior managers* – Review presentations by each manager to enable the entire group to rank critical issues and establish broad strategies.
- *Sales, marketing, and operations teams* – Evaluate the firm's strategic position in the marketplace, to establish its strategic intent and branding.
- *Finance and accounting team* – Develops more extensive strategic plans, with long-term financial projections.
- *Executive team* – Develops an annual operating plan and budget for the coming fiscal year.

By taking deliberate steps in the overall planning process and by involving key people at each phase—rather than having planning take place only behind closed doors—Goodmans is increasing the probability that the resulting plans will generate consensus and enthusiasm by the entire team.

## Using The Seven Questions Framework

How often should you refer to The Seven Questions for your business?

Think of it this way: Your answers to the long-term, strategic questions provide a sense of positioning, direction, and presence, and so these questions tend to be the type that have longer-term answers. Strategic initiatives at this level exist because of the strategic forces at play in your industry. The faster these forces tend to change, the more frequent the need to address these questions.

Operational questions tend to deal with the present time frame and operate at ground level. This level of focus deals with how efficiently you do what you do to optimize the results you seek. Operational efficiency deals with the execution side of the business.

I find more and more that businesses seek the right questions to guide them toward the right answers. It is important and easy to print your answers to The Seven Questions on your wall in the form of your mission, vision, values, goals, and so on. But these answers provide the results of your thinking at only one point in time.

## Summary of Operational Efficiency Questions

The questions *What, How,* and *When* are the questions that come to people's minds most frequently. These are the operational questions we wrestle with daily. Paying attention to these questions will help us execute our mission, vision, and long-term goals.

Adding the question *Why* to the operational questions gives people the context they need in which to thrive. Providing a purpose for achieving stated goals and objectives gives greater meaning to our daily existence.

## Key Lessons of This Chapter

1. *When* represents the dimension of time. Whether applied to the time frame for developing long-term vision and goals or to the action-oriented reality of here and now, the question *When* gives greater context to each of the other six questions in The Seven Questions.

2. The question *When* enables you to set expectations for your business in the context of a timeline. This implies that your business will always remain fluid and dynamic in an ever-changing marketplace. For this reason, always remember to examine how your answers to The Seven Questions will need to be adjusted to the changes that occur in the real world.

3. For most businesses in this country, and perhaps around the world, the current credit contraction is causing organizations to reevaluate how they will survive and grow. Demands for business growth, expense reduction, increased security, and rapid communications may very well affect the strategic intent of your business, let alone your market strategy, organizational design, and execution strategies. Remember to take the time you and your team need to rejuvenate. This means planning for an executive retreat where you can formulate a fresh vision and mission, set long-term goals, and determine how to strengthen your team and execute operating plans.

## Actions to Take

1.  Identify the subjects of your three most important goals. For each goal, determine how you will measure your success. Then establish the time frame in which you will achieve each of those goals.
2.  Include time in your schedule to reflect on your business strategy and what needs to be adjusted. Write down your most critical initiatives.
3.  Decide what you are willing to change for you to achieve what you really want.

## Congratulations!
## You Have Mastered The Seven Questions

You have challenged yourself with asking the toughest questions about your business. Here's a summary of what you have accomplished:

1.  You have reexamined your niche and alternative **choices** and have gained new insight into *which* business to be in, *which* market to target, *which* products and services to sell, and through *which* distribution channels to sell them.
2.  You have examined *why* you are in this business and the **purpose** and motives behind your thinking, and have clarified the key decision criteria you will use in making your most important decisions.
3.  You have explored *where* your industry is headed, where your business is headed, and where you want your future market **position** and vision to be.
4.  You have looked into the soul of your business and you clearly understand *who* you are in your industry in terms of your brand and the key **people** who set the tone, culture, and identity of your business.

5. You have come to conclusions on *what* **results** you want to accomplish, have identified critical areas for achievement, and have set major long-term goals and annual objectives.
6. You have explored the **process** of *how* you will achieve your goals and have identified key strategies that will help you to be successful.
7. You have decided *when* to place your plans in **action** and have determined the timing and sequencing of activities to fully execute your plans.

Now it's time to focus your intention and grow your business!

**The Results You Create
Depend on Your Clarity.**

# SECTION IV

---

## FROM STRATEGY TO RESULTS

*"You cannot change anything in your life with intention alone, which can become a watered-down occasional hope that you'll get to tomorrow.* **Intention** *without* **action** *is useless."*
—Carolyn Myss

Thus far, Section II of this book has focused on the strategic elements, and Section III has addressed the operational elements of The Seven Questions. You may also be contemplating how to bring this all together in order to begin implementing the concepts you have learned. Section IV was written specifically to help answer some of the questions you may have in taking action on your plans. Here is what you are about to read:

## Chapter 9: Executive Summary

This provides a very brief recap of the most important concepts of each chapter so you have it all in one place for handy reference.

## Chapter 10: Implementation

This is a bonus chapter for those who want more specific guidance in putting it all together and moving forward. It describes the delicate process of building consensus for *how* to get your entire team on board with strategies to grow your business.

## Chapter 11: Dig Deeper

Here is a second bonus chapter of inside secrets to help you develop your ability to ask the right questions.

## Chapter 12: International Applications

For those who work with executives from others cultures, this chapter translates The Seven Questions into selected languages and reveals the commonality of interest in answering these questions, regardless of nationality.

# CHAPTER 9: EXECUTIVE SUMMARY

*Always bear in mind that your own resolution to*
*succeed is more important than any one thing.*
—Abraham Lincoln

## Review of Key Concepts and Charts

Let's briefly list the key concepts in the book, which are reinforced with corresponding charts throughout the book.

These key concepts can guide you through your own strategy development and help you decide which areas need the most attention for your specific situation. Here is a summary of implementation ideas so you can begin taking action.

### Chapter 1: The Elements of Intention

**The Seven Questions Framework**            *(See Page 15)*
Use this planning framework to have your team diagnose the nature of issues in your company. Are your issues strategic or operational, and which questions lack clarity? After diagnosing which areas need attention, have your team develop answers to each question in order to focus your intention.

**Critical Issues Management**            *(See Page 25)*
Among the issues your business faces, determine which ones pose a substantial threat to the performance of your business or may otherwise have a great impact. Most likely there are only a few. Then, identify your strategic options, choose which initiatives to roll out, and build your strategic and operating plans from there. This will increase the probability that critical issues are resolved and your business will grow.

## Chapter 2: Which—The Element of Choice

**Strategic Choices**                                    *(See Page 29)*

Identify the critical choices your business faces in relation to targeted market segments, product lines, distribution channels, strategic alliances, and so on. By identifying which method of growth provides the best returns on capital with reasonable risk, you will determine whether to add new products or pursue new market segments.

## Chapter 3: Why—The Element of Purpose

**Decision Matrix**                                      *(See Page 50)*

For each key choice facing your business, identify the alternative strategies and evaluate these alternatives against your own decision criteria. This will help your team determine which alternatives hold the greatest potential value to your company.

## Chapter 3: Where—The Element of Position

**Competitive Positioning**                              *(See Page 66)*

Determine the criteria on which your company will be compared with your competition. Rate your company and your key competitors against these criteria, from your perspective as well as from the viewpoint of the marketplace, which may not be the same. Ensure there is a sustainable basis on which the market can differentiate your business from your competition.

**Force Field Analysis**                                 *(See Page 69)*

Identify the major external and internal forces that have an impact on your business. Your intention here is to ensure you have considered the entire context within which your business operates, with the intention to manage those forces you can influence. The more knowledge you have about your industry and issues within your company, the more equipped you will be as a leader.

## Strategic Intent *(See Page 73)*

Craft concise mission, vision, values, goals, and strategy statements that communicate your intention. These are not the typical flowery statements you read on the walls of most companies, but instead memorable statements that have an impact on customers, employees, and investors about your intention.

### Chapter 4: Who—The Element of People

## Progression Planning *(See Page 83)*

Evaluate who is ready to promote now or in the future and develop candidates for progression to key positions. Determine each individual's stage of readiness based on their skill level and experience.

## Leadership Assessment *(See Page 86)*

Determine the individual, interpersonal, functional, and strategic leadership skills of your key executives. This is not a typical performance review by the boss, but instead a broader view of key aspects of leadership, as viewed from the leader's subordinates, peers, superior(s), frequent contacts, and the leader's own perspective.

## Authority Matrix *(See Page 91)*

Identify who is responsible for making key decisions and when input from other parties is requested or required. This matrix can be helpful to clarify the responsibility and accountability of executives, managers, committees, and the board of directors.

## Chapter 5: What—The Element of Results

### Goal Setting (See Page 107)

Clarify the results you desire, along with specific metrics and time frames for achievement. This is a list of the top ten criteria you should consider in formulating your goals and objectives.

### Storyboarding *(See Page 110)*

A picture says a thousand words. Create a picture for your audience if you want to communicate how your business might look in the future. The *sample* storyboard shown illustrates how to broaden a concept into a business platform.

### Strategic Equity *(See Page 111)*

Increase the value of your company by identifying your company's brand equity, human equity, alliance equity, and systems equity. Once you identify where you stand today, work deliberately toward strengthening each component of strategic equity.

## Chapter 6: How—The Element of Process

### Business Development *(See Page 121)*

Determine how new business is referred to your company for each type of product or service your company sells. This should include referrals from customers, alliance partners, and other centers of influence. Also identify where the sale of one product or service leads to the sale of other products and services.

### Strategic Alignment *(See Page 124)*

Once your strategic intent has been crafted, seek to align every facet of your organization to this intention. This includes aligning your business to the needs of your targeted market segments, aligning each department to your company's intention, and also ensuring that the position of every employee is aligned with your mission, vision and goals.

**Organizational Alignment** *(See Page 126)*
Link all aspects of managing people to your strategic intention in order to ensure congruency. This includes the design of your organizational structure, job descriptions, employee objectives, performance reviews, compensation practices, and career planning.

**Content, Process, and Impact** *(See Pages 130-131)*
Once it is determined *what* to communicate, devote significant energy to enhance *how* the message is delivered in order to have maximum impact. If you want to impress your customers, employees, and investors, pay special attention to the process you use in order to create more impact.

### Chapter 7: When—The Element of Action

**Flow Charts** *(See Page 141)*
Determine the sequence of one activity to another in order to establish an overall schedule for your initiatives. There are many methods to increase the effectiveness and efficiency of key projects. Deploy a system that works for your particular situation to complete projects on time.

**Planning Retreat Design** *(See Page 167)*
First determine what is to be accomplished and then whom to invite. Then determine the process and setting to ensure the highest quality result. *(This chart is referred to here as part of this Executive Summary and discussed further in Chapter 10.)*

# Chapter 10: Implementation

*Successful people ask better **questions**, and as a result, they get better **answers**.*

—Tony Robbins

## How to Build Consensus

In Chapter 7 I discussed the importance of process in creating an impact. Even if you were to create the best answers to the questions in this book, that doesn't necessarily mean you will create an impact. The key to creating an impact is to design a process that builds consensus with those expected to carry out your plans. This includes management and employees. If you have a board of directors, consensus includes the board as well. So how do you build consensus?

Because I work so frequently with board and executive teams, this is the most frequent question I am asked. Here's my answer.

To me, consensus does not mean agreement. I often have cases where members of a group do not agree, yet I am still able to achieve consensus and get the group to move forward.

I define consensus-building as a process whereby all members in a group have the opportunity to express their viewpoints and be heard by others, understand the general direction a group wants to take, and are willing to support that direction.

This does not require agreement. What it does require includes:

- Listening carefully and respectfully to each person's viewpoint, regardless of their position.
- Understanding the pros and cons of each view and expressing a proposed resolution.

- Calling for consensus—which means "I understand and I am willing to support the proposed direction"—while respecting the right of individuals to personally disagree.
- Ensuring that after a decision is reached, all members continue to support the group's consensus and do not attempt to sabotage that direction after a meeting is adjourned.

Using this definition and approach, it becomes far easier to enable a group to move forward while respecting everyone's personal views. It allows for an individual who doesn't particularly agree to say to the rest of the group: "While I don't agree with everything, I appreciate your willingness to hear my opposing viewpoint, I understand where the team wants to go, and I am willing to support this direction within my department and with others."

I have found that simply by extending the courtesy of listening carefully to each person's viewpoint, the likelihood of achieving consensus is far higher. Further, if consensus cannot be achieved, I find that it is not based on a difference of viewpoint about business strategies. Rather, consensus is most often not achieved when there is a strong disagreement about personal values.

For example, if there is a lack of agreement about an aspect of integrity—such as misrepresentation to investors, or not being honest with customers, or tricking employees—then consensus is most likely not possible, and for good reason.

In my thirty years of consulting, I have had only two cases in which a CEO or chairman asked me to divulge highly confidential information. I stated that, ethically, I could not do so. It would compromise my personal commitment to professional ethics. When these individuals told me that I either needed to comply or would lose my consulting contract, I respectfully responded that we would not achieve consensus and I elected to disengage from the assignment.

These examples are extreme. Usually when a proposed action endorses the values of a company and respects the views of those involved, consensus can be achieved.

Building consensus also requires someone to facilitate discussion. Whoever the facilitator is, it is difficult to wear both the hat of facilitator and the hat of content provider at the same time. If you are the president or CEO, choose which hat to wear. If you want to engage in discussing the merits of a particular strategy, suggest someone else take the role of facilitator.

If the subject matter is extremely critical, you may elect to engage an outside facilitator whose role is to ensure that consensus is being built. Whether you use an internal facilitator or an external one, that person's role is to ensure that all parties are heard and the meeting objectives are accomplished.

## Define Your Starting Point

Many clients ask whether they need to apply The Seven Questions in a particular order, or the order in which this book presents them. The answer is no. The starting point is not as critical as ensuring that all answers to your questions are aligned in order to maximize the value to your business.

Some companies begin with clarifying answers to *why* they are in their particular business and clarifying their purpose and company values. Then they move on to other strategic discussions by addressing *which, where,* and *who*. Other companies begin by examining *how* they have performed against their annual operating objectives before thinking ahead in time and setting new goals.

You should tailor the process and sequence of addressing issues to your specific situation. If you are in a quandary of where to begin, here's my general advice as guidelines to consider:

1. **Identify and manage your most critical issues.** These are opportunities or threats that pose a substantial impact on the long-term viability and profitability of your business. It is your job to figure out *which* issues are most critical, so you can develop strategies of *how* to manage them. Be sure to seek the input of your closest advisors and your management team to make sure you are dealing with real, meaty issues. If you fail to identify the right issues, the strategies you develop may not have as strong an impact as you desire.

2. **Think strategically before thinking operationally.** Clarify *which* business you are in based on the ultimate value received by your customer and the position your business has in your industry. Express *why* you are in this particular business and define *where* you are positioned. Communicate *who* you are as a brand. If you are not sure of your position, ask your key customers what they think. Try to avoid just reading your own marketing literature and discussing this internally. You may find you are being myopic and not being brutally honest with how the market sees your business.

3. **Set goals, develop strategies, and take action.** Define *what* you want to achieve in the context of strategic position. Express *how* you will achieve it, *who* is accountable, and *when* to take action. Since operational efficiency deals mostly with *how* to provide your product or service better, faster, or with greater profitability, first be sure you are in the right business

with clear strategic intention. First be a leader, before being a manager.

## Before Conducting a Strategy Retreat

Before deciding to conduct a strategy retreat, first ask yourself the important question *Why?* Creating clear answers to The Seven Questions is important. So if you are an entrepreneur starting a business, there's no need to go anywhere. Just figure out your own answers.

On the other hand, if you work with a group of people on whom you rely to make the business successful, I indicated earlier that the process of building consensus may help you create a stronger impact. Inclusion of key people is important. You can definitely achieve consensus through a series of short in-house meetings.

Going offsite for a strategy meeting has its advantages, which this chapter goes into in more detail shortly. Strategy retreats can be conducted with the support of an outside facilitator or not. Know this: You do *not* have to spend money to begin clarifying your strategic intention; you just need your brain and your ability to engage others important to you.

If you plan on having a strategy retreat, identify the purpose of the retreat first. Then formulate answers to the next question, clarifying *what* is to be achieved as an outcome. To do this, be sure to gather input from those who will attend the meeting. If you do not consider their views, they may attend your meeting while they are practicing their golf swing in their own mind.

We have all experienced boring meetings that simply waste everyone's time. If you decide to hold a strategy retreat, make sure you are doing everything to ensure a successful outcome. Since strategy meetings deal with critically important issues, avoid the risk of meeting failure.

## Focus on Strategic Choices

Section II of this book purposely starts with the question *Which*, because that is most often how The Seven Questions is used in actual strategy retreats. Begin your meeting by identifying the choices you are facing. This approach, while not required, has its merits.

Most businesses today struggle with *which* market segment to target and *which* product or service to develop. Making substantial progress on this subject early in the planning process provides momentum to complete the answers to all other questions. It helps all those involved feel that the purpose of strategic planning really is to make a huge impact and not some academic exercise that wastes their time. This discussion of issues that are most critical engages an audience very quickly.

The process of identifying alternatives and choosing among them applies to every question. I know it is easy to forget that we truly do have choices, even if we are not aware of them. Being able to make choices promotes a feeling of being in control. By becoming more cognizant of the choices we make, we are far more likely to keep our business on track with our values and goals in order to get what we want. Being aware of alternatives and making choices is empowering. Groups do well when they feel empowered. Your retreat will start with positive energy if you recognize that your business has many choices.

## Process Considerations in Retreat Design

It always happens. I am invited to facilitate a retreat where the participants have already been invited, the retreat site is set, and all they want is someone to facilitate the retreat. And there is no agenda yet. This is a red flag.

Similar to business strategy and organizational structure, the questions of *Who, How* and *When* must always be sequenced after *Why, Which* and *What*. Specifically, *Why* is the meeting being held? *Which* issues are to be addressed? *What* do you intend to accomplish? Clarifying answers to these questions first will lead you to *who* should be invited, *where* the retreat should be held, and *when*.

Retreat design is "issue contingent." Begin by determining which issues are critical. Determine who should attend by the nature of issues to be addressed and potential attendees' knowledge, insights, and leadership on the specific issues.

Determine the best setting for the type of retreat you are holding. Identify the information that will need to be discussed. All other considerations, even the arrangement of chairs in the conference room or whether to meet outdoors, must flow from what you intend to accomplish.

## Create the Right Setting

*How* do you ensure the right environment for reflection on your answers to The Seven Questions? Begin first by asking yourself where you and your team would feel most comfortable addressing business issues. What is the best setting for your team of executives, board members, or advisors to contemplate the future of your business?

Most likely the best environment for a retreat would not be in your corporate office. Use of your office may prompt operational issues to be discussed and can result in many interruptions. Consider the benefits of going away from the environment that you are in daily. If you want fresh thinking, go to a fresh environment.

Consider the following questions:

- *Which* environment would yield the best outcome?
- How much travel time should you allow?

- Would the retreat be an overnight event?
- *What* is the total budget you have for your event?
- Should there be time to socialize?
- How long should your retreat last to achieve the desired outcome?
- Should there be one big event, or a series of smaller events to provide "gel time" between major activities?

## How to Facilitate a Successful Retreat

Begin by conducting a situational assessment that results in a laundry list of potential issues. After completing this step, group issues into "buckets" that naturally fit those issues.

For example, clients frequently group issues into strategic, financial, operational, cultural issues. This is just an example. Don't force your issues into these labels. Group issues by whatever "buckets" they naturally fall into.

After you have all the grouping of issues laid out, determine which group of issues you want to tackle in the retreat. Once you select which issues the retreat should focus on, determine the appropriate process to deal with the issue.

The Planning Retreat Design chart is helpful in understanding how to proceed from issues identification to strategies.

This model demonstrates three steps in resolving any issue:

1. First, there needs to be consensus on the nature of the *issue* itself. This means agreeing on the right question. If there is disagreement on what the issue is, there is little hope that the right strategies will evolve from a retreat.
2. Before commencing strategy development, be sure to identify the right *process* to be deployed. This means determining *who* should be involved, *how* the strategies will be developed, and *what* resources will be needed.

## PLANNING RETREAT DESIGN
Identify *Which* Issues to Tackle
Before Deciding *Who* Participates

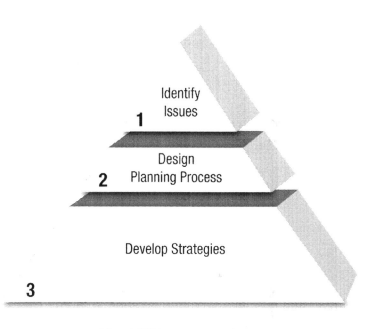

© Copyright 2009 Strategic Development Corporation

3. If, and only if, steps 1 and 2 are clear, you can proceed with **strategy development**. This represents finding answers to the right questions.

The primary objective of the retreat is to ensure there is executive, or if necessary, board consensus on the nature of the issues. Given that boards and executive teams often see issues from different perspectives, it is in your best interests to develop consensus on identifying the most critical issues of the company.

Once the subject matter has been chosen, discuss the cause and effect of each issue. *What* drives the issue and *how* does the issue manifest itself in symptoms and bottom-line company performance? This will help you understand both the magnitude of impact the issue can have on your business and the sequence of *how* and *when* the issue should be addressed.

Here's an example of sequence: If one of the issues you have is deciding *which* business to be in and another issue is organizational design, it is best to decide first *which* business to be in before tackling the organizational design of *how* to achieve the best results in that business.

## Wrapping Up Your Retreat

Before your strategy retreat adjourns, be sure to wrap up with a clear listing of where you go from there. This means clarifying:

- *What* major actions are to be taken from this point? *What* major milestones will represent that progress is being made?
- *Who* is accountable for executing the next steps?
- *How* will the process unfold for actions to be taken?
- *When* are results expected, and in what form will they be communicated?
- *Who* will convey the retreat results to those who did not participate?

There have been times when I have taken executives on a strategy retreat to explore market positioning or potential acquisitions. During this time, the executives found out that employees were wondering if the executives were discussing who would be laid off.

Don't allow this mistake to occur! Communicate openly why executives or managers will be gone and afterward, what results were achieved at your retreat. If you fail to do this, employees will fill in the blanks with their own perceptions, which may create an additional issue for you to resolve.

# Chapter 11: Dig Deeper

*Judge a man by his **questions**,*
*rather than his **answers**.*

—Voltaire

## Questions Have More Power Than Answers

I have studied and coached CEOs for so long that I have come to some interesting conclusions about the impact that leaders have.

Many executives have demonstrated brilliance in their strategic positioning by crafting and executing the strategies to grow their business. I have certainly appreciated working with such incredible talent.

I have been more impressed by leaders whose expertise lies in their ability to identify the right questions to drive their team's thinking. They give the credit to their team for their success and give little credit to themselves. This is fascinating to observe and I have learned a great deal from these leaders and the enthusiasm they generate.

My impression comes from the comments I hear from the management team about their company's culture. They feel alive, valued, and appreciated. They never feel bored. Behind all this is one phenomenal leader.

Become that leader. Improve your ability to ask the right questions. Your team will discover a whole new meaning of being motivated to create compelling strategies.

## The Best Questions Cause Deep Thinking

Great questions tend to be *open-ended;* they cannot be answered with yes or no. In strategy retreats, when I ask a team to define their critical issues, I ask them to identify the open-ended question that needs to be resolved. Suggesting this ground rule causes deeper thinking about an issue. More important than the subject matter, a great question frames the work to be done.

I find that the best questions are *generative*. This means they evoke other questions that drive even greater thinking. A generative question can begin with, "What would it take to _____?" Here are some examples of generative questions that lead to other questions:

- "What would it take for us to become the undisputed leader in our field?" Someone may add to this question with "How can we build a competitive advantage that is the envy of every competitor?"
- "What would it take for every single customer to willingly refer two more customers to us?" This may lead to "How can we create a benefit to customers for referring business?" or "What would be the single most important thing we could do to delight our customers?"
- "What would it take for our stock value to double every year for the next five years?" Other questions that relate to this could be: "Which new subscription services would our customers be compelled to sign up for on a long-term basis?" or "Which types of acquisitions would make our value proposition more compelling every year?"

Initiating your process with generative questions is likely to frame additional questions that help the management team dig deeper to develop strategies.

*Become fascinated with **questions**.*
—Max Dixon

## The Art of Combining Questions

As demonstrated in Chapter 2, combining the question *Which* with the question *Why* in the form of a matrix creates a decision-making tool. This is a simple but powerful tool that can help ensure you are making the right decisions for the right reasons.

Many of my clients benefit from determining which set of questions belong together for their specific situation. Here are some examples:

- *Which* are our most important criteria and *why*?
- *What* are we going to accomplish by *when*?
- *Who* will become the next generation of leaders and *how* will they acquire the right executive experiences?

You get the idea. Often clients create a spreadsheet to list their answers to a set of two, three, or four questions for the purpose of generating clear strategies. All you have to do is observe which questions your team wants answered to achieve clarity.

Here's a quote that is not particularly business-oriented, but I had to laugh at the author's humor in asking multiple questions.

> *Where am I? Who am I? How did I come to be here? What is this thing called the world? How did I come into the world? Why was I not consulted? And if I am compelled to take part in it, Where is the director? I want to see him.*
> —Soren Kierkegaard

If all seven questions were to be used, the last sentence might be converted to another question such as "*Which* world is he in and *When* can I see him?"

## Repeating the Same Question

In Chapter 3, it was demonstrated that repeatedly asking the question *Why* can yield greater insight. This technique of digging deeper can also be applied with other questions as well.

One of my clients wanted to be deliberate in making careful *choices* in defining their best opportunity. Here's how they continued to refine their questions:

- *Which* markets and market segments should we pursue?
- *Which* submarket segments hold the greatest potential?
- *Which* customer demographic would be willing to buy our product?
- *Which* distribution channel should we select for this demographic?
- *Which* industry organization does this type of customer have a membership in?
- *Which* of our salespeople have the most experience with this market segment, customer demographic, distribution channel, and industry organization?

Their meeting ended with a very specific action plan for selected salespeople to pursue their ideal customer types and a strategy for doing so.

> *Computers are useless.*
> *They can only give you answers.*
> —Pablo Picasso

## Convergent and Divergent Thinking

Your ability to generate the answers you are seeking is directly affected by your ability to ask the right questions. This takes practice.

To build your skill in finding the most compelling question, there are several approaches you can take, including the two just presented: (1) selecting a set of questions to be answered in the form of a matrix, and (2) repeatedly asking the same type of question, such as *Which* or *Why*. These are examples of *convergent* thinking—bringing all resources together to "converge" on a specific subject.

Another way to think of this is what I call asking questions at the "ground level." When working with my clients, I find that executives tend to ask questions that address such topics as improving sales, strengthening profitability, improving the satisfaction of a given client, or deciding who will take action next week. There is nothing wrong with these important questions. The issue, however, is whether there is a more critical question that has gone unnoticed or unresolved.

A different approach is to continue to step back and up to a "higher altitude" from the situation and practice *divergent* thinking—generating ideas for alternatives.

Divergent questions might include topics such as: Which other businesses could we be in and why does this one make the most sense? What other products or services might our customer want to buy from us? What would be the most significant alliance we could create to propel our business?

As Chapters 2 through 5 demonstrated, these types of questions focus on strategic effectiveness. By asking such questions, you may find you are exploring the potential of new markets, products, technologies, and delivery channels. Discussion of these topics will yield the most expansive, divergent thinking. Brainstorming like this holds substantial value.

An easy analogy to distinguish between the two: divergent thinking is a green-light brainstorming session for the purpose of innovation; convergent thinking is a red-light session for the purpose of decision-making.

You may find that after a green-light brainstorming session, your team has covered all four walls of your conference room with ideas. Be sure to complete the process by converging on the best questions and ideas in the room. It is often the case that out of fifty ideas, only one, two, or three hold incredible potential.

> *As a leader, one of the most important tools at your disposal is a well-worded question. Critical to leadership success, questions beg for an answer, focus your thinking, get people talking, make you listen, control the answer, get people to persuade themselves, and give you control.*
> —John B. Spence, Author
> *Excellence by Design: Leadership*

## Balancing Strategic and Operational Issues

After identifying critical strategic issues that could either "make or break" a business, many of my clients realized they were spending insufficient time addressing these strategic issues.

Companies that were most successful in making progress on critical issues devoted either weekly, biweekly, or monthly meetings to monitoring critical strategic matters. The frequency of meetings focusing on strategic matters can certainly be relaxed once the most critical issues have been resolved.

A good rule of thumb is the more strategic and critical the issue, the more attention is required.

Some companies purposely schedule executive strategy meetings for times other than when they meet on operational matters. This enables group accountability on sticking only with strategic discussions. Otherwise, most people tend to resort to questions like "Did we ship that order to customer X last week?" and not questions like "What would it take for us to secure 80 percent of the market?"

In short, if you have a meeting on strategic matters, stick to the subject and channel any operational issues to the proper forum.

### Case History in Structuring Meetings

A major supplier to the aerospace industry routinely scheduled senior management meetings every Tuesday morning and had done so for years. But when the executives concluded that a multitude of strategic issues were *not* being addressed effectively in these meetings, they decided to alternate the agenda each week from operational issues to strategic issues.

In each week's meeting, the CEO kept with the agenda of being either a strategic meeting or an operational meeting. When subjects came up that were outside the purpose of the meeting, the CEO tactfully channeled that subject to the following week's agenda.

After a full year passed, the management team was so delighted with their progress, they decided to continue the habit so their skills in strategic issues management would continue to grow.

### Accountability for Issues Management

Other companies assign executive accountability to a senior person to manage all facets of a critical strategic issue. Such an issue might be accountability for developing a strategic alliance, merger, acquisition, new product or service, culture, executive succession plan, incentive compensation plan, or research and development. Having clear accountability for a significant issue helps avoid finger pointing. If an issue is critical, someone needs to be held accountable for managing it.

Does your company now have any such mega-issues? If so, which issues are they and who is accountable? How are these issues being discussed and reported? Are the right people involved in resolving the issue? Are the people who are expected to carry out the initiative engaged in building consensus? Take critical issues management seriously, and you will be delighted with how much progress is made.

## Funding Your Business

Over the years I have been asked to review hundreds of business plans. Each time, I do so by using the framework of The Seven Questions to check the clarity of the plan. If the planner has not adequately addressed these fundamental business questions, it becomes quite evident. Conversely, when I observe great clarity in the answers to these questions, these plans portray a strong executive team. Be sure your intended audience gets a clear message quickly, without having to hunt for answers.

Entrepreneurs who prepare business plans to present for funding by venture capital firms, angel investors, and banks are well served to use The Seven Questions as a framework. If they fail to answer basic questions, you can be sure their plan does not generate the enthusiasm they were hoping to achieve.

Don't worry about what you call the results you want to achieve, whether company goals, objectives, or targets. What you might call company values, others companies call guiding principles. Mission statements sometimes include vision and goals as well. The labels you place on your strategic intent statements are relatively unimportant; the content of your words is vital. As long as you present your answers to The Seven Questions in concise terms that are compelling and memorable, your audience will be impressed.

## The Seven Questions Audit

The Seven Questions can be used to conduct an audit of strategic and organizational effectiveness. You can run this process yourself for your company, although sometimes it might be helpful to engage an outside professional.

I want to share with you how I run this process so you can gain insights on an approach. Here's how the process works.

I begin by interviewing key executives and asking a variety of basic questions to understand the situation. All of these questions are not necessary to get a full picture, so I generally ask a few open-ended questions and then keep quiet and listen carefully. Here's a sampling:

- What concerns do you have?
- What keeps you awake at night?
- What does your company do extremely well?
- What causes your company to lose business to competitors?
- What do you like best about this company?
- If you could change one thing, what would that be?
- Why did you join this company?
- Are you having fun?

My interviews are as simple as that. I am also careful to not "lead the witness" by engaging in specific strategy issues. Doing so will cause the interviewee to talk more about subjects they *think* I want to hear about, but this biases the interview.

When appropriate, I also interview board members, outside professionals who provide counsel or service, key customers, and whoever can help me form a complete picture of the situation.

I also review as many materials about the company as reasonable, including but not limited to:

- Financial statements
- Budget variance reports
- Strategic plans, if available
- Operating plans and objectives
- Management biographies
- Customer feedback
- Marketing literature
- Research reports
- Industry journals

In addition, I always conduct an on-site visit of their plant or branches whenever possible. In particular, I like to see the offices of executives, which tells me a lot about the individuals. Books they read, pictures on the wall, trophies they have won, placement of furniture, and every detail reveal how they view their role in the company.

All of this is leading somewhere. When I have completed all of my due diligence, I prepare my own summary using The Seven Questions. This helps me determine the nature of issues present.

Perhaps the company has had difficulty making strategic choices. They might be in the wrong market or might have developed products for their target market that are not selling. Sometimes they have an excellent product, but use the wrong distribution channels to sell their products.

Each of the symptoms the company may be experiencing can be sourced to a question that has not be addressed effectively, or has been avoided altogether. This insight gives me a hint of how the company might improve its performance. I then review this analysis with the CEO to confirm whether my hypothesis is confirmed.

Using what I refer to as The Seven Questions Audit, I am generally able to find areas of opportunity and can make recommendations. The CEO is then in a better position to determine which areas, if any, call for further assistance.

In all cases, my audit results are meaningful to the CEO. Sometimes it confirms a nagging feeling the CEO had about a problem. At other times, it serves as reassurance that what was perceived to be a problem is only a symptom manifested by some other issue.

During the last 25 years at Strategic Development Corporation, I have had only two cases where my report was perfectly "clean." This means I was unable to uncover any substantial issues that warranted the attention of a strategy consultant. One case was a clothing retailer, and the other was a food manufacturer. In both companies, the CEOs were delighted that I concluded they were doing fine and that I honestly believed they were *not* in need of consulting services.

Conduct your own assessment using The Seven Questions Audit. Determine where your issues lie within this framework. This will give you additional insight into how to focus your intention and grow your business.

# Chapter 12: International Applications

*It is better to know some of the questions*
*than all of the answers.*
—James Thurber

## Translation to Other Languages

My quest for more understanding of the art of questions led me to explore this topic in other languages. In many languages, but not all, the literal translation of each of the seven English questions is also a one-word question.

Some European languages have single words to convey the question *How much?* such as *Cuanto* in Spanish, *Quanto* in Italian, *Combien* in French, and *Wieviel* in German.

In the English language, the question *How much?* consists of two words and conveys an expression of the quantity of result. This is similar to the question "to *what* level?"

The importance is not the wording of the question itself—*What* or *How much*—but instead, the meaning behind the question (i.e., the subject of achievement). Helping you achieve clarity of your intentions is what this book is all about.

## The Interest in Questions in Other Cultures

Over the years I have consulted with executives who are Italian, Swiss, Dutch, French, Swedish, Spanish, Indian, Chinese, Japanese, and Native American.

Regardless of nationality, culture, gender, or age, people throughout the world have the same fundamental desire for clarity in their answers to these questions.

This is because every culture has the same inherent interest in choices, purpose, position, people, results, process, and action.

For this reason, The Seven Questions as an integrated strategy model has the potential to become ubiquitous because these questions have served humanity throughout the ages and cannot be replaced. As long as people continue to have interest in the fundamental elements of intention, the framework will always be of value.

| ENGLISH | SPANISH | ITALIAN | FRENCH | PORTUGUESE |
|---------|---------|---------|--------|------------|
| Which? | ¿Cuál? | Quale? | Quel? | Qual? |
| Why? | ¿Por qué? | Perchè? | Pourquoi? | Por que? |
| Where? | ¿Dónde? | Dove? | Où? | Onde? |
| Who? | ¿Quién? | Chi? | Qui? | Quem? |
| What? | ¿Qué? | Che cosa? | Ce qui? | Que? |
| How? | ¿Cómo? | Come? | Comment? | Como? |
| When? | ¿Cuándo? | Quando? | Quand? | Quando? |

| ENGLISH | GREEK | DUTCH | GERMAN | RUSSIAN |
|---------|-------|-------|--------|---------|
| Which? | Ὁποιοι; | Welke? | Welches? | Который? |
| Why? | Γιατί; | Waarom? | Warum? | Почему? |
| Where? | Πού; | Waar? | Wo? | Где? |
| Who? | Ποιοι; | Wie? | Wer? | Кто? |
| What? | Τι; | Wat? | Was? | Что? |
| How? | Πώς; | Hoe? | Wie? | Как? |
| When? | Πότε; | Wanneer? | Wann? | Когда? |

| ENGLISH | JAPANESE | SIMPLIFIED CHINESE | TRADITIONAL CHINESE | KOREAN |
|---------|----------|--------------------|---------------------|--------|
| Which? | どれか。 | 哪些? | 哪些? | 어느것? |
| Why? | なぜか。 | 为什么? | 為什麼? | 어디에? |
| Where? | か。 | 在哪里? | 在哪裡? | 어디에? |
| Who? | だれか。 | 谁? | 誰? | 누구? |
| What? | 何か。 | 什么? | 什麼? | 무엇? |
| How? | いかにか。 | 怎么? | 怎麼? | 어떻게? |
| When? | いつか。 | 何时? | 何時? | 언제? |

# APPENDIX

---

# Solution to Thinking Outside the Box

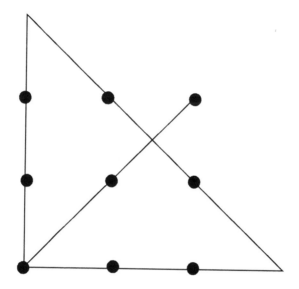

# ADDITIONAL RESOURCES

Strategic Development Corporation has launched a series of initiatives designed to provide you and your business with additional support for implementing The Seven Questions program.

### The Seven Questions Speaking Engagements
Speaking engagements are provided for corporations, industry associations, professional organizations, universities, chambers of commerce, and government organizations.

### The Seven Questions Seminars
Educational seminars for medium to large audiences are available for presentation to just one company or a mixed audience brought together by a sponsoring organization.

### The Seven Questions Strategy Retreats
Confidential executive and board retreats are conducted for clients as a means to generate substantial progress on either a specific issue or several related issues. These offsite retreats are used by clients either to diagnose the underlying source of issues or to develop strategies to resolve an issue.

### The Seven Questions Software
Strategic Development has begun designing planning software to help CEOs and entrepreneurs plan their business. This software will assist businesses and organizations in developing strategic business plans and tracking progress against these plans.

### The Seven Questions Certified Strategy Consultants
Strategic Development (www.StrategyCounsel.com) is building a network of consultants who use The Seven Questions as a

proprietary diagnostic and planning tool. Consultants must have significant experience in corporate strategy and be trained by Strategic Development in order to receive certification.

## TheSevenQuestions.com Website

This website will continue to grow to feature products and services specifically related to The Seven Questions. In the near future, it will also provide a forum to raise additional questions on business strategy and receive online feedback, advice, and counsel. A feature is being created to showcase the best examples of strategic intent created by companies. This will help generate new business for those who participate.

## The Seven Questions Book Series

Clients and associate consultants have asked me to publish a short series of The Seven Questions books targeting specific groups who have a high need for question-based planning frameworks. The following books are in the queue for further consideration and development.

### The Seven Questions for Business Growth

This book you are reading represents the first of an intended series of books and materials focusing on business growth. Materials are currently being prepared to focus on the special interests of board members, entrepreneurs, investors, and professional service providers.

### The Seven Questions for Personal Growth

Intended for the personal growth sector, this series could include applications for career changers, families, married couples, college students, and high school students.

At this time, Strategic Development is focusing on the business market, which represents our core expertise. We are also engaging in joint venture discussions with other providers that specialize in the personal growth market. The Seven Questions model is being extended beyond books to software, educational games, online services, and a host of related products.

# RECOMMENDED READING

## Strategic Planning

- *Strategic Planning* by George S. Steiner
- *Strategic Planning for the New and Small Business* by Fred L. Fry and Charles R. Stoner
- *The Mission Statement Book* by Jeffrey Abrahams
- *The Survival Guide for Business Families* by Gerald Le Van
- *Turn Strategy Into Action* by Terry Schmidt

## Marketing Strategy

- *How to Grow A Profitable Business* by Frank Cooper
- *Navigating the Partnership Maze* by Sarah Gerdes
- *TechnoBrands* by Chuck Pettis
- *The Discipline of Market Leaders* by Treacy Wiersema
- *The Long Tail* by Chris Anderson
- *Upside-Down Marketing* by George R. Walther

## Leadership

- *Entrepreneur America* by Rob Ryan
- *Fire in the Belly* by Sam Keen
- *Good to Great* by Jim Collins
- *It's Not About the Coffee* by Howard Behar
- *Leaders: The Strategies for Taking Charge* by Warren Bennis and Burt Nanus
- *Leadership Made Simple* by Ed Oakley and Doug Krug
- *Excellence by Design: Leadership* by John B. Spence
- *Leading Change, Overcoming Chaos* by Michael L. Heifetz
- *Pour Your Heart Into It* by Howard Schultz
- *The 7 Habits of Highly Effective People* by Stephen Covey
- *The Pursuit of WOW!* by Tom Peters
- *Walk the Talk, and Get the Results You Want* by Eric Harvey and Alexander Lucia

## Presentation Skills

- *10 Simple Secrets of the World's Greatest Business Communicators* by Carmine Gallo
- *Speak and Get Results* by Sandy Linver
- *The Communications Catalyst* by Mickey Connolly and Richard Riansoshek, Ph.D.

## Mind Power

- *Change Your Thoughts—Change Your Life* by Dr. Wayne W. Dyer
- *The Book of Secrets* by Deepak Chopra
- *The Power of Focus* by Jack Canfield, Mark Victor Hansen, and Les Hewitt
- *The Power of Intention* by Dr. Wayne W. Dyer
- *The Seven Spiritual Laws of Success* by Deepak Chopra

# BUSINESSES REFERENCED

# INDEX

*A Letter from the Author*

This book is all about *you*—the entrepreneurial executive, a leader who identifies new opportunities to delight customers, energize employees, and attract investors.

Want better answers? Try better questions. *The Seven Questions of Business Strategy* distills strategic thinking into an easy-to-use, powerful framework. Strengthen your ability to identify issues critical to your business. Clarify your strategic intent. Build consensus with your executive team on how to fuel growth.

Consider this book *your personal guide to strategic thinking*— a catalyst that stimulates insight. Encourage your senior managers and closest advisors to dive into these concepts with you. Capture new ideas that emerge. Boldly explore compelling strategies to ignite your business.

Discover the power you have in focusing your intention. Your customers, employees, and investors will thank you.

Your strategy counsel,

Norm Levy
Founder & CEO

(888) 900-0727 toll free
www.StrategyCounsel.com

# ABOUT THE AUTHOR

Norm Levy has served as founder and CEO of Strategic Development Corporation for more than twenty-five years. He has also served as Interim CEO of Loctronix and Greenopia, CEO of Ansyr Technology; CAO of CourtLink; vice president of corporate strategy of Seafirst Bank; and management consultant with Touche Ross.

For more than thirty years, Norm has provided counsel to executives and boards of directors on business growth strategies. His clients have included industry leaders such as Starbucks and Boeing, as well as successful small businesses and start-up companies.

Norm is a member of the National Speakers Association, National Association of Corporate Directors, and Northwest Entrepreneur Network. He has served as president of the Puget Sound chapters of The Planning Forum and Planning Executives Institute. The Institute of Management Consultants Pacific Northwest Chapter has honored him with its Outstanding Member Award.

Norm has lectured on corporate strategy in programs sponsored by Washington Software Association, American Electronics Association, Washington Bankers Association, University of Washington Graduate Business School, Seattle Pacific University, and Antioch University. He earned his M.B.A. at Cornell University and his B.S. in mechanical engineering from Rutgers University.

Norm and his wife, Denise, live in the foothills of Mt. Rainier in Washington.

# TO ORDER ADDITIONAL BOOKS

For online orders,
*visit* **www.Amazon.com**

For volume purchases and discounts,
*visit* **www.TheSevenQuestions.com**


## FURTHER INFORMATION

For consulting services,
*Go to*: **www.StrategyCounsel.com**

To contact the author directly,
*Email*: **Norm.Levy@StrategyCounsel.com**

To call Strategic Development Corporation,
*In Washington*: **(253) 863-0727**
*Toll free*: **(888) 900-0727**

6170391R0

Made in the USA
Lexington, KY
25 July 2010